SHE POURS

A Book Compilation Anthology

Printed in the United States of America

First Edition, 2024

PAPERBACK ISBN: 979-8-3305-4700-5

HARDBACK ISBN: 979-8-3305-4702-9

EBOOK ISBN: 979-8-3305-4701-2

Red Pen Edits and Consulting

www.redpeneditsllc.com

DEDICATIONS

To the women who pour into the lives of others, your strength, your love, and your wisdom are a gift to this world. You are the quiet forces who uplift, guide, and empower, often without recognition, yet your impact is immeasurable. Whether through the nurturing of children, the mentorship of young minds, or the support you offer to friends and strangers alike, you are the heartbeat of communities everywhere. You take your lived experiences—both the joy and the struggle—and transform them into lessons that light the way for others.

This book is for you—the mothers, daughters, sisters, mentors, teachers, leaders, and caregivers—whose unwavering commitment to others creates ripples of change that span generations. You show us that true strength lies not in what we keep for ourselves, but in what we give away, freely and without expectation. You teach us that resilience isn't just about surviving, but about rising, again and again, to offer more of ourselves to those who need it most.

May your efforts never go unnoticed, and may you always find the love and support you so generously offer to others. Your selflessness is a reminder to the world that compassion is the most powerful force we have, and the future is shaped by the hands of those who care.

This book is a tribute to you. Thank you for pouring into others and making the world a brighter, kinder place for all.

TABLE OF CONTENTS

INTRODUCTION

In every corner of the world, there are women whose lives reflect the unspoken power of generosity, wisdom, and empathy. These are the women who, despite facing their own struggles, take time to uplift, guide, and inspire others. They pour into the lives of those around them—whether through their families, careers, communities, or personal relationships. Their actions and words are a blend of strength and softness, grounded in the knowledge that life's challenges often reveal our greatest potential for growth, not just for ourselves, but for those we choose to serve.

This book is dedicated to exploring the stories and experiences of these extraordinary women—those who give so much of themselves to others, who pour from their own reservoirs of lived experience into the lives of people around them. Whether it's a mother raising children in the face of adversity, a mentor guiding young professionals through their career paths, or a community leader rallying people for social change, these women leave lasting imprints on the hearts and minds of those they touch.

Through their lived experiences—sometimes filled with pain, other times with triumph—these women offer more than just advice. They share a deep and resonant knowledge that only comes from navigating the intricacies of life. Their wisdom is not just theoretical; it is forged in the fires of real-life circumstances, shaped by failures, resilience, and the courage to rise again. As they pour into others, they offer not just solutions, but a profound sense of hope and understanding, a belief that change, growth, and healing are always possible.

The stories of women who pour into others are deeply rooted in the power of lived experience. Life is full of trials, challenges, and moments that shape who we become. And it is through these moments that women find their voice—the courage to speak from a place of authenticity and to share the lessons learned in the process. Whether it is a woman who has overcome personal loss, battled with illness, or fought against societal barriers, her experiences have shaped her into someone who not only survives but thrives and reaches back to help others along their journey.

What makes these women particularly powerful is not just their ability to give, but their resilience in continuing to give even when they have been drained. The reality is that women who pour into others often face the same emotional, physical, and mental fatigue that any caregiver or provider experiences. The weight of their responsibilities can sometimes feel overwhelming. Yet, they continue to show up—not because they are invincible, but because their sense of purpose drives them to pour out even when they feel they have nothing left to give.

This kind of resilience is not born from an absence of vulnerability, but rather from the understanding that vulnerability and strength coexist. It is in the moments of fragility that these women find their greatest strength—not in a desire for recognition, but in a deep commitment to the well-being of others. Through their acts of service, they demonstrate that true strength is not always about physical power or stoic endurance; sometimes, it is about showing up with an open heart, offering compassion even when it feels hard to do so, and trusting that in doing so, they will receive what they need in return—whether in the form of gratitude, connection, or the knowledge that they have made a difference.

This book is not only about celebrating the women who already pour into others, but also about inspiring a new generation of women to do the same. The world needs more women who are willing to share their wisdom, their strength, and their compassion. It is a call to action for women of all ages and backgrounds to recognize the power they have to influence, to guide, and to nurture.

In the pages that follow, you will read about the journeys of women who have poured into the lives of others in profound ways. From mothers to mentors, entrepreneurs to activists, these women have made a lasting impact through their actions, their words, and their love. Their stories serve as reminders that even the smallest act of kindness or mentorship can set into motion a wave of change. They show us that by pouring into others, we pour into ourselves, creating a world where compassion and empowerment are limitless.

In the end, the power of a woman who pours into others is not measured by the number of people she helps, but by the deep and lasting change she creates in the hearts of those she touches. As you read their stories, may you be inspired to pour into someone else, to offer your time, your wisdom, and your love, and to become part of the beautiful, transformative ripple effect that these women have set in motion.

She Pours!

Alicia Harris Pours

Alicia Harris LPC LPC-S LAC
Email: Boldbaldgurl06@gmail.com
Facebook: Pieces A Soulful Journey with Alopecia
Instagram: Pieces_asjwa

My name is Alicia P. Harris and that P stands for Patricia. I was named after my mother. I was born in Brooklyn, New York and grew up in East New York. Then, my family and I moved to Camden, New Jersey. I have a lot of fond memories from Camden. Nowadays, not many people positively reminisce about Camden, but back then, Camden was a pretty decent place to live.

My grandparents had a two story house. It was the type where the doors were side by side versus on top of each other. These were my paternal grandparents. They lived on one side. My mom, my dad and I lived on the other side. I'm the only child that was a product of my mother and father's marriage and I was the youngest of five children. I remember having a dog and nice neighbors. My grandfather would take me to the Acme Supermarket in his Pacer. Yep! That's how old I am. We rode in a Grey Pacer. And then, one day, my little oasis was disrupted. My parents separated and ultimately got a divorce. That ripped a part of me that I seemingly never recovered. It took a long time to get over. What happened? I don't know all of the details because I was a kid. I do remember the locks being changed on our door. This was to prevent my mother from getting in when she returned home from work one evening. There was a lot of loud screaming and I didn't understand why my mother couldn't get into the house. After that, there was a vicious battle between my mom and dad. My mother wanted custody. Do you know how they tell kids to stay out of grown folk business? I was that kid sitting on the stairs and listening to the adults talk about adult business. I wasn't supposed to hear. I was completely heartbroken that, now, my oasis, as I knew it, was utterly destroyed. My mother won custody of me and that uprooted me from Camden, New Jersey and moved me to Paterson, New Jersey.

My mom is from South Carolina. That's part of the reason that I'm here today. My mother didn't go to high school. If I recall correctly, she may have had a sixth or seventh grade education. In that, she was trying to navigate the world, with me in tow during a very rocky situation. I grew up in the Grand Street Projects in Paterson, New Jersey. They no longer exist now. This was a culture shock for me. I went from living in a home, seeing my grandparents every day and having family dinners to this concrete jungle. The only person that I knew there was my mom. I had to figure things out. I made some friends, but I also experienced bullying at a young age. Bullying back then was nothing like it is today. I longed to go back to my safe place in Camden, New Jersey. The projects taught me a lot about growing up and surviving.

Now, I was always a smart kid. I was the "go to school on Saturday" smart. Trust me! It wasn't because I wanted to. My brother went to school on Saturdays too. My mom was trying her best to survive in a new environment and keep me alive. So, my brother just plugged me into anything positive. I couldn't understand it and I resented it. However, hindsight is still 20/20 and I have more of an appreciation now than at the time. As a child, I had a lot of aspirations and dreams. The one thing that I longed for and didn't have was my father, his approval, and his love. It's not that I didn't see him anymore. My aunts were instrumental and intentional about ensuring I interacted with my family.

In our community, and even after desegregation, one thing still existed in the black community: colorism. My mother was a beautiful, chocolate woman in a petite 5' 2" frame. I called her a keg of dynamite. My dad was a very handsome, fair skinned, black man at 6 feet and 3 inches with hazel eyes. My grandparents looked like two little white people. My grandmother really despised my mom because of the color of her skin. That really did something to me and it was my first experience with being exposed to family hating on each other. We're all black, but because of her skin color, she was hated on. She was instrumental in the separation of my parents. In my mind, "you split up my home."

My dad was a mama's boy and he did what his mama told him to do. My grandmother was very instrumental in destroying that part of the family unit for me. Thankfully, my aunts kept in touch with me and made sure that I was still engrafted into the family. I wasn't cast aside. However, they didn't know some of the hardships that I was experiencing with my mom. I lived based on the mantra, "What goes on in here, stays in here." No matter how hard it was, I couldn't speak about it. No matter how many times we didn't have food, it was nobody's business. No matter how many times we didn't have lights, I had to keep quiet. No matter how things worked out, I had to show face. You don't tell anyone. I became the bearer of that burden. I knew that if I told anyone, my mom was going to lose me. That meant that I was going to have to go back to my dad. My aunts weren't there. They were social workers in Dyson, New Jersey. Remember now, I was a kid. I was hungry and we didn't have lights, and I couldn't reach out to them for help. Doing that meant that my home was going to be disrupted. My mom would be angry with me. My mom would lose me. I had to show face and do what I had to do.

I can remember those times with my mother. She worked every day, but she wasn't good with her finances. All of that was coupled with me growing up in the projects and being a latchkey kid because my mom was always at work. She instructed me to go into the house and not open the door for anyone. She was very explicit about these directives. She didn't care if it was Jesus at the door! Do not open the door! That's how I grew up. I had the fear of God in my life. As a matter of fact, I believe that I feared my mother more than I feared God because I didn't know any better. She would call the house to make sure I was in there and then she would get home when she got home.

To reiterate, my mother was not good with money. There were times when we were without a place to stay. We had to stay with friends or whoever we could find. In my upbringing, it was a common thread to be without. Well, we weren't completely without, but something was always lacking. If we had a roof over our heads, we may not have had lights. If we had lights, we may not have food. It was always something.

We moved from Camden to Paterson and lived in the projects. We got evicted from the projects and moved across town to a house that was like an apartment. Some of the landlords would rent out houses as apartments. This one was on Graham Avenue in Paterson. I think they renamed that street Martin Luther King Boulevard. We lived there for quite a while. There was still a sense of uncertainty. Are we going to have food? Will the lights be on?

Then, came my teenage years. I got pregnant at the age of 16 in high school. Right after that, I think my oldest daughter was probably two or three months old, and we got evicted from our place. I had to stay with the family of my daughter's father because my mother didn't have anywhere for us to go. I felt displaced. I didn't know my living arrangements from one minute to the next. Am I going to be here? Am I going to be there? What about next week? Have you thought about next year? I was clueless. I graduated from Eastside high. Mr. Clark, the real Joe Clark, was the largest figure in my life and may have saved my life. He was so intentional. He knew every child's name in that high school. If you were walking down that hallway, and you were late, you were going to sing the same "Fair Eastside" to the seniors. He didn't care. Expeditiously will always mean something to me, because that was his word. "Let's get the class! Move expeditiously! He made a huge impact on my life. As a pregnant mother, I didn't have to go to the main high school. We went to a different high school so we didn't have to walk up and down all of those stairs. I left during my junior year because I was pregnant with my daughter, but when I came back, he picked up where we left off. "Alicia, are you doing what you are supposed to be doing? Stay on track so you can graduate." I valued his impact and impression on my life. Some people tried to discourage me by saying I would never be anything coming from Paterson, New Jersey. The thought I would just have babies and be on the system. Mr. Joe Clark was like, "No, that doesn't have to be your story." So, I stayed there, graduated, and met my first husband.

You may want to pack a lunch for this next part of my story. Let's go down this road. When I met my first husband, I was 17, and he was like 20 or 21. Yes, he was older than me. I was growing up in the inner city, and here is this dude. He has a car. He is nice looking, and he's interested in me. Don't forget. I have daddy issues. I want my dad's approval and his love. My dad was in my life, but he wasn't in my life. My desire to see others not experience what I have been through comes from the lack of pouring from my dad. I don't want people to feel like they have to buy love or perform to receive my support. My dad was the most inspirational person from a lacking perspective, but positively, my most inspirational person was my Aunt Rose. Aunt Rose is my dad's sister. If it had not been for her, I wouldn't have had a relationship with my dad or my father's family. She was that person. She was at birthday parties. She was at graduation. Whatever I was doing, she was there. She took me on vacation. She purchased my school clothes for the new school year. Aunt Rose was very instrumental in making sure I maintained high family values.

Family values mean a lot to me. I want my kids to feel loved and hear me say it to them. Far beyond words, I want my kids to feel the touch of my arms and I hug them. I'm not only a safe place for them, but I have their back. When I think about my core value, I think about legacy and what I want to leave behind. When I close my eyes, what do I want my kids to say? Not that I gave them a bunch of money. Not that I took them a bunch of places, but that they can remember me wrapping my arms around them and letting them know, I'm here and I want to be here!

My pour is based on the needs of the people. It is very similar to how I pour into my children. I have three kids and they're all adults now. All three of them have different personalities. When you ask my oldest daughter a question, she's going to give you answers A and Z. My son is going to give you answers A through Z. My youngest daughter is going to provide you with answers A, G, T, and Z. Over time, I have learned to pour based on what they needed and not what I wanted. That's what I do with everybody that I am connected with, from families and friends. I want to pour what you need. There's no need for me to pour you soda when you need orange juice. I strive to be intentional in my pour and not the cookie-cutter type.

My relationships are based on the need, the dynamics, who the person is and the sense that my actions are genuine. Trust and believe – all of my relationships have not fared me well. There's an old saying that says, *"nice guys finish last."* For a long period of time, I thought in that same manner. I have always been a giver. I've always been an advocate for the underdog. I want to see fairness for everyone. Sadly enough, there are people out there who take advantage of your kindness. My ex-husband was one of those people. He capitalized on it in a negative way. In that relationship, I experienced domestic violence in every way possible: physically, verbally, and mentally. It was so bad that it almost cost my life because, on more than one occasion, he tried to take it from me. Because of his actions, I sought to hide the nice and friendly person. I resorted to being the "I'm going to get you before you get me" person. I refused to let anyone ever mistreat me again. I became an angry and easily agitated person. I would fight at the drop of a dime, and I acquired a self-proclaimed Ph.D. in profanity. This became my shield. I threatened people that I would cut them, and they feared being stabbed with a knife. Contrary to popular belief, I didn't have a knife, but I possessed an even sharper tool and it could rip your entire world to shred. That tool was my tongue. I prided myself on that.

This went on for years and into my second marriage. It's not a good look to go into a new relationship without healing from the past. Hurt people, hurt people. Broken people, cut people. I was broken, and I was a danger to myself and others. I didn't realize that, and it prevented the current Alicia from coming forth. I was afraid to show vulnerability out of fear that people would take advantage of me again.

Then, I met Valerie ?....

Valerie was my spiritual mom. I had just transitioned from New Jersey to Virginia. I still had this New Jersey residue on me and I Valerie and her husband at the time who was a Pastor. He would go out and evangelize and I thought he was a book salesman. Needless to say, I joined their church and gave my life to Christ. Valerie was the person who said many people don't approach me because of my exterior, but she was going to jump in the ring with me. She acknowledged that underneath my hard shell was a kind and loving person. She also mentioned that she was not afraid of me. She was the first person to tell me that and, in that moment, I could feel layers breaking off of me. I felt an overwhelming sense of peace in that moment. I felt that she wasn't going to do me any harm. I felt like she wasn't going to abuse me. It was help that allowed me to be rebirthed and re-introduced as this new version of Alicia.

I love this version of Alicia. I struggled with blaming myself. I struggled with self-esteem and self-worth. Why did I allow that to happen? Why did I let them treat me like that? Things got bad and my life was toxic, but through my relationship with Valerie and my spiritual growth in Christ, I experienced a newness in life. I learned so much from Valerie including how to value myself, how to have a better outlook on life, and how I was designed. I learned that my trials and situations don't have the power to dictate how I show up in life.

Then, I met Dr. Stephanie Kirkland...

I went through her six-month program and more issues were revealed to me. I had unresolved daddy issues. I was a people pleaser. Now hear this.... I'm a therapist and I help people daily, but I had to have a moment of reckoning wherein these issues were exposed and resolved. I thought I had dealt with it. I even had to deal with the fact that I had alopecia. I was so ashamed of how people would look at me. In my final speech to the class, I said that I came into the class with hair and I was walking out bald.

I can remember it so vividly. The Lord spoke to me directly and said that He wanted to deal with the alopecia. I was like, "Nope. I'm good!" My locks were always up. I went to the doctor for a CT scan for my sinuses and I told the doctor that I couldn't take my locks down and then the bobby pins had to stay in. Who does that? That was six years ago and I shaved those locks off. That was one of the most freeing and liberating events of my life. I cried the entire time.

My oldest daughter was there. She inquired, "why are you crying?"

I lashed out at her. "You have hair and I don't. You don't understand."

She replied, "everyone has something that they are going through. Yours is just visible."

For a moment, I was angry but then, I finally realized that God, like only He can, beautifully connected all of these things together to create this person that was once meek, mild, timid and insecure into this beautiful, bold and bold woman. From there, I wanted everyone to come into their level of acceptance and authenticity. That's where I am personally.

I've done a lot of work to deal with a lot of toxicity and generational and generational curses. I've done a lot to make sure that my kids have opportunities to express themselves in the areas that they feel like I fell short as a mom and to repair relationships. I told my kids, that I don't want to leave this earth with them feeling stuck with issues that they couldn't talk to me about. I allow them to speak freely and they allow me to apologize because I didn't do everything right, I was making decisions through a broken lens. I explained that when you're broken, you make broken decisions. You attract broken people, and you think that you're whole. I'm thankful that I've had the opportunity to mend those areas with my kids.

I'm the little black girl from Paterson who nobody thought would amount to anything but churning out babies and living on welfare. Now, I'm about to be Dr. Harris. Although my mom didn't have much education, she drilled in my head to make sure I got that "doctory" degree. She couldn't say doctorate. She said "doctory". Iwas like, "Yes, ma'am. Yes, ma'am." I wanted to be a medical doctor. I wanted to be a surgeon. Life started life-ing and I thought I was grown. I didn't want to go to college for the rest of my life. God is so faithful and He is the God of second chances. I may not be a medical doctor, but I am still a doctor and I am going to help people.

I'm shocked at the opportunities that open for and to me. Some days, I'm like "God! You got to be kidding me." I'm honored when I'm called upon to speak and be in unexpected spaces. I'm honored when the Attorney General calls upon me. I'm overwhelmed with gratitude because didn't have to do it. I'm convinced that if He does nothing else, I can truly say that I have been blessed. My kids see it and my grandkids see it.

Now, here is another reality. The calling and assignment on my life comes with a cost and sometimes, I don't want to pay the cost. However, with everything, there comes a cost. Even doing nothing, cost something. Which one will you choose? The legacy I want to leave behind requires me to do something.

God is a redeemer, not only of time, but of circumstances. No matter where you are in life - It may look like it's over, or the dream won't come true, but God can redeem anything if we allow Him to.

Cherish your family. You don't have to raise your kids the way you were raised. I'm not saying anything is wrong with it, but everything isn't right with it either. Know what is needed of your children, or your family and hold that close. Out of all the accolades that I have, my biggest accomplishment is that I've raised three awesome children, who are positive contributors to society. That's it. I don't care how much of an alphabet soup is behind my name. It's all about making sure I raise three awesome kids.

Be good to yourself. So many times, we as women, become martyrs. We take care of everybody. We want everybody to know that we're taking care of everybody, but there is no reward in self-neglect. Take care of yourself. If you're not the best version of yourself, you're really cheating yourself, and everybody else.

I want to make sure that as a black woman, our stories are told. We all have a story. Sometimes, without knowing another woman's story, we judge them. We judge prematurely. We judge harshly, and we don't afford grace. I believe that as black women, there's so many obstacles that we have to overcome. If we, as a community of women can come together and love on one another, listen to each other stories and find hope, inspiration, and afford grace, at least we have one safe space in that we can exist.

Tiffany Myers Pours

Tiffany Myers: Caregiving & Transformation Coach
Minister, Speaker, Motivator
Website: https://tiffanylmyersconsulting.com/
LinkedIn: http://linkedin.com/in/tiffany-l-murphy-8abb9a3a
Instagram: tiffanysunshyn
Facebook: Tiffany Myers
Email: info@tiffanylmyersconsulting.com

Who am I? That is a loaded question. I am a vessel. What does that mean? I am the person that will impact you without you knowing that you needed to be impacted. I am the person who will tell you the truth without you knowing that you needed that bit of truth. I am the person that will shake you when you didn't even know that you needed to be shaken. I'm the person who will slap you with that white glove because you've been lying to yourself or you've been in a shell or you've been masking something. I'm the truth-teller.

My name is Tiffany Myers. That's who I am. I am a wife of over 20 years. I am a mother. I am a friend. I am a sister. Overall, I am the person who will come to you, look at you directly in your eyes and ask, "what did God say about it?" Not what did Tiffany say about it? Not what did you say about it? Not how do you feel about it? Not what did you do about it? But what did God say about it? That's who I am. I am the person who will hold you accountable, even if you didn't ask me to. However, if you open your mouth or if you open up, or even if God prompts me to, I'm going to hold you accountable.

I am a caregiver coach. That just started in the last couple of years because my husband had a lung transplant. I had to take care of him part-time since 2018. It got really, really bad a couple of years ago because the doctors said "no, he's not going to have to have a transplant" and then turned around and said "Oh, you got to have a transplant." After a tug-o-war battle with Charleston, I decided to be his caregiver. I'm already a certified life transformation coach, but being a caregiver is a nuance that people don't even think about. We just had COVID. We just had a lot of people, young and old, being sick for absolutely no reason. Oftentimes, we think about respite care and Alzheimer's or accidents. Rarely do we think about the caregivers of their child who may have a degenerative disease. They may have a mental illness. They may be caregivers of their parents. They may be in that position by default because they drew the shortest straw, or they are the most responsible person. I am a wife and a caregiver and I have come to realize that there is a voice that caregivers don't have. That's why I became a caregiver coach. People look at the person that is sick, but the health of caregivers declines too because they don't take care of themselves. They're not well and they don't talk about it. They don't have a voice, so I became a caregiver coach.

I am a published author and a mother of sons. I published a book of love letters to my sons called Dear Sons. One day they sat in the kitchen at our house and told me how they felt about how I raised them. After I got out of my feelings, I decided to write a book because my sons needed to see me better and not bitter. The book talkd about how I was sorry about what I did and why I raised them the way I did. It also prompted other people to look at themselves, their relationships with their children, and things that they did in their past that may have impacted them. Furthermore, it prompted thought-provoking questions. What are we still doing? What are we still tied to? What curses do we have? What bitterness do we have in our hearts, that we're still carrying into other relationships and not allowing us to have genuine, true relationships? That's why I wrote that book.

I am a friend. I am a sister. I believe people need someone to count on. If I'm your friend, I'm your friend. I'm going to be there just as thick as a blood relative. If I call you friend, I call you friend. If I call you, sister, I call you sister. Some people need to be embraced. Some people just need a hug. Some people just need someone to talk to and you are not there physically. There's no better feeling than the feeling of being held up. They may not be in your house, but you feel them. They may not be in your local area, but you can feel them holding you up. That's accountability.

My pour was greatly influenced by my mother and my grandmother. They both taught me the art of selflessness. My mother was a quiet force. She was prim, proper and dainty. She had a heart of gold. Even with all of those timid qualities, she was also forceful, powerful, and impactful. When she walked into a room, she warranted attention effortlessly. She encompassed beauty. My grandmother was the same way. They loved with that agape type of love. People loved them. They didn't know a stranger. Because they helped people feel loved, people gravitated to them. They exuded love. They poured love. They demonstrated love. This also includes my dad. My parents showed love to everyone. I can remember my parents going to check on people when they were sick and when people came to our, rarely did they leave empty-handed. My parents would easily say, "Oh! You're about to leave? Let me give you something" and then proceed to empty our freezer to ensure they had food to eat. That was a defining dynamic of my family. My dad loved to cook. His brothers loved to cook. His sisters loved to cook. Now, as for me and my house, when you come to visit, you better bring something so we can all eat. Evidently, I missed the cooking trait. Some things skip generations.

God allows and affords me an opportunity. One thing I have learned in the past is that you can't pour into everyone. That can be detrimental to both parties. My pour is a God-pour. He instructs and directs me to who I need to pour into. God gives me the wisdom, wherewithal, and strength to pour the way I do.

My pour can be very exhausting at times, but what keeps me going and pouring is the fact that I don't have a choice. My life is not just mine. Don't forget – I'm a vessel. Vessels are used for a purpose. One thing that you will always hear me say is that "What I do, what I say and how I am is because my life depends on me." I have to be obedient. At times, there are risks. I have to be quiet. I have to pull back to myself for the purpose of spending quality time with God to hear from Him. Yes! It gets exhausting, but that's when I pull on His strength. Everybody and everything is not my assignment. Every place is not my place to go. Everything is not my thing to do. It takes obedience to operate in my type of pour. Sometimes I can cheer people on from the sidelines. Then, there are times when I have to sit down. Sometimes, I have to take a back seat and sometimes, I need to get involved. As a caregiver, I need to be well in order to serve. If I'm not well, I can't help someone else to be well. In that moment, instead of ministering, I need to be ministered to. Take a break. You can't go to that event. Take a nap. You can't accept that invitation. Read a book. Turn the phone off. Don't answer the door. Consider the concept of being "unable to can".

Can you say that? I am unable to can.

You know what's sad? Someone just read that laundry list of suggestions and that declaration and created an excuse to not do any of them. To that person, I offer my sincerest wishes and in the spirit of Hallmark, I say, "Get Well Soon".

I believe that more people need to exercise one of the most impactful, powerful, and shortest sentences in the English language. That sentence is "No!" No is a powerful word. No is a sentence all by itself. No is a response. The fact of the matter is this. I don't owe anyone an explanation when, where, why, and how I place my No.

So, I am a caregiver coach. I come in contact with many caregivers who are exhausted in their work. There are a lot of things that you can do to replenish yourself. I would like to suggest that you intentionally take five minutes every day to simply be. Don't think about what is next or what you have to do later. Take this time for yourself. Take some time to eat. You would be surprised to hear the amount of caregivers who forget to eat on a daily basis. Don't just eat. Eat something healthy. Eat something that can provide you with the fuel you need to get back to the assignment. Some other things that you can do are budget and find your support system. I'm going to dispel one rumor right here. In some cases, your support system will not be in your phone contact list or have the same last name as you.

Here is an example of the importance of this intentional five minutes. During this journey of caregiving, I encountered this lady whose husband had a double lung transplant. Her husband was very sick. On the Thursday before Easter, I can remember standing with her face to face and holding both of her hands. I said to her, "inhale and exhale" because she wasn't breathing. I told her, "You husband can't breathe, but you're not breathing."

When she intentionally took a moment to breathe, she exhaled everything that was weighing her down and her immediate reaction was to cry. She inquired, "Where did you come from?"

I responded with something that I have mentioned in this chapter more than once. "I am a vessel." She needed that. She needed to breathe.

In this journey of caregiving and my reasoning to pour, I know of loved ones who are sick but they worry more about their caregiver than they do about themselves. They can see that you are tired. They can see that you are depleted.

My influence to be a caregiver came from my grandmother. She unselfishly and I saw her take care of her mother, which was my great grandmother. My great grandmother was a midwife from Bluffton in the Kershaw County area. My great-grandmother had dementia. She was over 100 years old. Over time, she started reverting to her childhood mannerisms and she transitioned at an old age. After my great-grandmother passed, my grandmother took care of my grandfather, who had lung cancer. These are the people that I came from and I learned the art of caregiving.

There are a few considerations that I want everyone to understand about my pour and the pour of others. I believe that everyone should respect everyone's pour. Some people under appreciate the pour of others. Sometimes people want your pour, but they don't understand the cost of your poor. They really don't understand. They can't fathom the sleepless nights. They don't realize the gift that comes with the pour or the weight, or the sacrifice. Obedience comes with a cost. If those of us that sincerely pour from a genuine place came together, it would create such a community of collaboration and creativity. That wouldn't leave any room for competition or animosity. We could accomplish so much more....together.

Respect the pour.

Respect your sister.

Respect your brother.

Respect the pour.

STERLIN BOYLES-GARDNER POURS

Sterlin Boyles
Instagram: @Cuffedcrownedqueen
Email: Easternstarsterlin@gmail.com
Email: Cuffstocrownsllc@gmail.com
Snapchat: fromcuffstocrown

My name is Sterlin Boyles-Gardner. I am originally from Newark, New Jersey. I was born and raised in East Orange. I moved to Columbia, South Carolina as a teen. My father passed away when I was middle school or high school. My mom decided that she wanted to move back home to Columbia and I've been calling South Carolina home ever since. I graduated from Lower Richland High School in 1999. I have three beautiful young adult children and a grandson. I am pursuing my Master's degree from Strayer University in Public Administration. As of recent, I've been maneuvering through life trying to figure out adulthood and raising children. Early in life, I made some poor decisions including being incarcerated. When I came home, I had to re-introduce myself to society. I teach my children to not do as I do, but to do as I say do. I've been participating in some modeling and acting gigs along with plus-size pageantry and successfully won six titles. That outlet allowed me to fulfill my passion of helping women like myself. Even more specifically, I want to help women get better acclimated to society after being incarcerated. Society doesn't make it easy for formerly incarcerated people. I seek to empower and assist women who have had bumps in the road and made some mistakes. Currently, I am in my 40's and I am the product of a praying mother and a praying grandmother. With their support, my children have not made the same mistakes that I made. I want to be a walking, talking, living example of possible change. It is difficult but it can be very rewarding.

South Carolina is home, but I also lived in New York and North Carolina for some brief times. Moving from New Jersey to South Carolina was hard. We lived on the outskirts of Columbia in Gasden which is down near Hopkins and Eastover. I went from the city life to the country life. I'm talking about walking down dirt roads and seeing deer in your front yard. It was a process coming down here, making friends, and getting adjusted. Making friends was hard because girls didn't like me. I was picked on because I was the new kid on the block.

Losing my dad was very tough. My mother and I grew apart and I decided to take another path in life. I guess I was attracted to the fast life. I watched movies like New Jack City and saw people living their best life with all of the fortune and fame. I wanted that. I met some people. I can't say that they were all the best for me. I had my first child at 15 years old and that was a crusher for my mom. She saw me as a smart young lady with a lot going for me, but then, I had a child in the ninth grade. Life threw me loads of lemons, but I didn't quite have the lemonade recipe perfected so I made some bad decisions that caused me to get incarcerated for two years. I came home on parole after serving a little under a year. Unfortunately, I wasn't able to secure employment. While out, they kept throwing restitution and supervision fees at me. Within a few months, I ended up going back to jail to finish my time because I didn't have the means to pay over $600 in fees.

Let me be clear. I made some serious mistakes. I had about eight felony convictions. I went to jail for scamming and cashing fake checks. I obtained some fraudulent information and I was opening bank accounts and cashing checks that didn't belong to me. Once it was investigated and we got caught, we had to do the time. I was accustomed to getting money one way. I went to jail and came home. I was trying to be on the straight and narrow under supervision. During that time, I was required to do community service and pay all of this money back to the financial institutions that I victimized. Here I am, smart and an honors graduate. I was capable of getting a good job, but I was being told "No" daily. What do you do when you have the qualifications to get something but you are disqualified because of your previous actions? When you are incarcerated and come home, there is a large amount of poverty that you have to endure. Depending on your charges, it will be hard to get a job.

My experience was a journey. I was in my 20's, making minimum wage at a fast food restaurant, and going through a separation from my ex-husband. I was only making $500 every two weeks. That's not a livable wage now and definitely not then. It was me and my three children. Talk about keeping your head above water. I was doing the best that I could. I thought to myself, "I'll just pay the restitution fees and worry about the supervision fees later." When you are on probation, there is still a price to pay and if you don't, there is another price to pay. Sometimes, you can have a parole officer who wants to see you win, and others will want to give you a hard time. During this probation, I was assigned to my second probation officer. She was not trying to give me a break at all. I tried to make arrangements to pay the supervision fees later but she was not having it. Her reply was that if I didn't pay by a certain date, she was going to send me back to jail. And that's exactly what she did.

I have a passion for women that are going through this same type of ordeal. It's hard to get reacquainted with society. Most women want to do the right thing. They want to get a job. They want to get their children back. They want to be able to support themselves, but the responsibilities of freedom can be too much. They want to go to school, but the system doesn't make it easy. They want to get a good job, but taxes will break you. I was acing my interviews, but when the background check was completed, I received more "No's" than "Yes's". However, I refused to settle. I had to pull my inspiration from somewhere.

My inspiration comes from a full list of people such as my children, my mother, my grandmother and my spouse. There were also a lot of people in the community. Some have transitioned on. These are the people that saw something in me that I didn't see in myself. Like, when I was incarcerated, I met a teacher. His name was Mr. Barksdale. He taught a computer class. When you are incarcerated, you will take every opportunity to prevent all day lockdown. From a cooking class to whatever extracurricular activity, you did whatever it took to just leave the building. So, I took Mr. Barksdale's computer class in prison. When I came home, I ran into Mr. Barksdale and he inquired about my next phase in life. I was just trying to make it , but he encouraged me to go back to school. With his support, I was able to get my Associate's Degree from Midlands Tech. When my son graduated from high school, Mr. Barksdale helped my son secure money for his college education. Then, he introduced me to Tammy Blount, who had a parenting organization. I explained my situation to her. This new connection helped me to buy Christmas gifts for my children and presented me with an opportunity to speak to women in the prison system. Now, that I think about it, that was one of my first opportunities to pour. From there, I went to D.C. to attend a conference and met so many people who were all about positivity. They wanted to see me win. They stressed the fact that my circumstances were not the end. I questioned myself. What do I want for my children? What do I want for myself?

By this time, I was in my 30's. I encountered some bumps in the road, but I was determined to get free from my criminal background. I was determined to make sure my children were good. I was determined to make sure that I had a better life for myself. All of these determinations seemed hard to attain, but my community and the people whose paths crossed with mine, helped me in a tremendous way. Now, my desire is to continue showing up. I'm going to PTA. I'm going to Open House. I'm going to the sporting events. I may have missed birthdays, btu I'm here now. I made mistakes, but I'm here now. My superpower is in showing up. I choose to show up for my children because I want them to know that I am proud of them.

Good job! You can do this! Let me help you to do better!

These are the words of encouragement that will go a long way. These are also the words that have built my platform to pour. I have encountered people that have helped me to get my feet on solid ground. I can't change what I have done. All I want to do now is find opportunities to serve. How can I give back? Where can I pour next? If I can help the mother who needs groceries, I'm going to Harvest Hope Food Bank to pack cars with food. If I can meet people from the Hanna House, I want to provide assistance and plant seeds of hope. I want to show people that this is not the end. My daily mission is to give where I can.

That's where I am in life. I'm revised, renewed, and reborn. I'm just trying to be a better version of myself today than I was yesterday. I'm a helper. I do a lot of work in pageantry. Due to health issues, I am operating more on the production side. I recently partnered with Big Homies, Little Homies for their Sneaker ball. I'm working with another organization where we collect toys for children of incarcerated parents. Due to my personal diagnosis with breast cancer, I am active with a breast cancer walk.

If I'm not pouring on my own, I believe in the power of collaboration. I want to be a voice for formerly incarcerated women. Where ever I can give back, pour back, and make life easier for someone else, I'm doing it. My pour is intentional.

Marquita Nesbitt Pours

Website: www.fs2s.org
Email: Marquita.fs2s@gmail.com
Facebook: From Struggle To Strength
Instagram: @frmstruggletostrength

My name is Marquita Nesbitt. I was born and raised in Asheville, North Carolina. I'm originally from the mountains, where it actually snows and not just dust like in Columbia. We have a blended family and I am the oldest of six. I have three bonus brothers and two sisters. It's more boys than girls, but I am the oldest of them all. I have two children: Kenneth, 20, and Isaiah, 17. Isaiah is a special needs child. He has a genetic disorder called Mosaic Turner Syndrome, which is a genetic disease. He only has one functioning kidney. He has had 4 major surgeries. He has two valves from his heart. I have spent a lot of time in and out of the children's hospital. He is also autistic but he is high-functioning. He's capable of doing a lot of things for himself. I'm considered a PK (preacher's kid) because my father serves as an Elder in the Church of God In Christ. I've been in church all of my life.

I moved to Columbia in 2012 so I could be closer to a specialist for my son. As opposed to traveling all over North Carolina, we ended up here in Columbia. My son's father moved from New York to Columbia before Isaiah was born. He knew the area a little bit so I thought it was going to be a good idea. The other option was Charleston, but I thought that was too far from family. I thought I would have the help of my son's father. However, I moved to Columbia with no family and with no help. I was doing it by myself. That's where I started to build my strength.

I also witnessed this type of strength in my mother. She is my inspiration. I grew up in a home with my birth mom and my stepfather. In that home, I saw abuse and sadly mistook it for love. He was terrible to my siblings. I saw my mother get up every day and work for 11-12 hours. She would walk to and from work because her husband would have her car. Her tenacity and perseverance have always inspired me. She made sure that we always had what we needed. She never complained. She never changed and she kept going. My mother epitomized the "in sickness and in health" vow. A couple of years ago, my stepfather was hit by a car. This accident left him brain-dead and in a vegetated state. After years of abuse at the hands of this same man, she made the decision to take him and care for him until he passed. My mother instilled in me to always take care of and show up for my children. She taught me that nothing in life will be given to me so it is imperative for me to work hard. I was also instructed to accept people for who they are and to help in any way possible regardless of the circumstances.

My pour is directed towards younger girls and younger women. I just turned 40, but for almost half of my life, that demographic has always gravitated to me. I love to help people. I've been doing this for 20 years. I want to help young girls complete school as a single mother. I don't care what your situation is. I always position myself to help and I position those who are connected to me, to win. That doesn't make sense to many people. Years ago, I allowed this older lady who was addicted to drugs to stay with me. Everyone had an opinion, but I was her safe place. She never stole from me. She never made me feel uncomfortable. And here's the thing – she wasn't from my family. How many times have you allowed a family member or friend stay with you and things came up missing? How many times did you leave them in your home and felt uncomfortable about what they may be doing in your absence? This is going to sound grammatically incorrect, but sometimes, it be your own friends and family. I didn't know what all she needed from me besides shelter, but whatever she needed, I positioned myself to provide. My acts of kindness gave her hope and she was further encouraged to get off drugs. That made my heart leap. You have to find purpose in your pour.

The purpose of my pour is to help women. Even more specific, I seek to help women from abusive relationships such as myself. My non-profit organization, From Struggle To Strength (FS2S) did start as an organization. From its inception, FS2S started as a story. My business mentor encouraged me to tell my story and implored me to share my story. The sharing of my story ended up in written form as a book called "From Struggle To Strength". Within the pages of that book, I shared my experiences with domestic violence and abuse in multiple forms. From its success, I created a business that assists women with getting free. Let me tell you this. Being free doesn't end when the abusive relationship ends. I figured that out. While writing my book, I cried and wrote some more. Then, I cried, felt layers fall off of me and wrote some more. I experienced levels of freedom and this was years after the abusive relationship was over. I thought I was free, but the freedom and liberty that comes from writing the details of your story is unprecedented. I ultimately gained strength from talking about the struggles I experienced during that time in my life. After telling my story, once again, my business mentor said, you should do more. So, I started my non-profit organization by the same name. I didn't create this organization just to have a non-profit. I successfully registered with the Secretary of State, acquired my 501c3 tax-exempt status, and created programs that will impact the community.

I pour consistently because somebody needs me. There is a declaration that churches recite and it simply says, "I believe that God is raising up somebody, somewhere, to use their gifts, talents, and abilities to bless me." Guess what? I am the somebody that God is raising up and through me and my organization, I want to bless someone. Someone needs my encouragement to push them to the next level. Someone needs my ear to listen to them. Someone needs my shoulder to cry on. I can't give up because when I do, someone's need goes unfulfilled.

That said, my goal is to open a transitional home for battered women and children. I want to purchase an abandoned hotel that includes all of the amenities in each room to provide a safe haven for those who seek refuge. I want to turn it into an apartment facility that offers programs for individuals to gain self-sufficiency. I want to include an on premise boutique so when the women and children come to the facility, they can get clothing. We will teach life skills, career, personal and professional development.

I had to learn that I was worth more than what I was going through early in my lfe. Then, I had to learn that I was more than just a book. Then, I learned that I wasn't your average business owner. I own an empire that will change lives for the better. My pour will assist women with moving from struggle to strength.

Engle Nicole Johnson Pours

Facebook: Engle N. Johnson

Instagram: @Engle N. Johnson

Email: johnsonengle@gmail.com

My name is Engle Nicole Johnson, formerly Moseley, but my maiden name is Johnson. I was born in here in Columbia, South Carolina. I have two beautiful children. My oldest, Miles Mosley, who I don't get to spend as much time with is 23. He's a grown man. He has grown into an awesome young man. He had some struggles during his high school years when his father, which is my ex-husband, and I were going through our challenges as a married couple. My son endured a lot of the dysfunction we displayed to our children. I really regret that. He is very independent, goal-oriented, and vocal about the things he learned from the challenges he witnessed in the relationship between his father and I. Recently, he complimented me for holding the family together in his younger years. He called me a woman of character. He has a CDL and he wants to become an entrepreneur through the building of a clothing line with his business partner. He's doing some wonderful things. I'm so proud of him. He is planning to give his first car to his sister, Kennedy, as he prepares to purchase his second car. That is so generous.

My pour originates from my childhood. Some childhood traumas aren't recognized until you've evolved and learned what childhood traumas really is. I have two grandparents that I could talk about all day. My maternal grandparents were the foundation of my family. However, they were unequally yoked. Meaning, a lot of the struggles in their marriage were due to an imbalance in communication, finances, and spirituality, just to name a few. Those things caused a dysfunction in their marriage. I grew up witnessing that. My normalcy included not showing affection. It was normal for me to not be vulnerable. I experienced co-exiting without a purpose. My relationship could have been defined as getting along just to get along.

My life is a roller coaster of ups and downs. I normally start my day at 5:30am. As soon as my feet hit the ground, I'm giving God thanks for another day. I wake my daughter up with some love and encouragement for the day. Then, I'm off to work where I am met with an array of challenges. Students stop by all day to talk during my planning period. I have a full schedule of responsibilities and professional obligations such as speaking with parents and administrative duties. And it doesn't stop there. We're just getting started. I have a class to teach and more students to interact with. In that environment, I'm mentoring....pouring. Many of the issues that I deal with are not about the student's education. I find myself pouring throughout the day at work. Oftentimes, my students tell me, "you remind me of my dad" or "you remind me of my mom" or "you act like so and so". I take those comments as compliments during my 8+ hours at the office. Then, I transform into my mom role as I journey home. And it doesn't stop there. Not only am I mother at home, but I am also caregiver as my 70-year-old mother lives with us too. Yep, you figured it out. We have three generations of women in one house. All females! Women Rock!

In doing and being all that I am called to do and be, I have recently learned how to take care of myself. I'm talking in just the past two years. I spend time with myself and do things that I enjoy. I realized that I have to do it for myself because rarely do I get it done by someone else. I try my best to create opportunities to escape. Every escape is not a physical location change. I escape in my mind. Exercising is therapeutic for me. I love pilates. It's so peaceful. It's only for an hour, but I make the most of that hour. I want to encourage everyone to get away. There is nothing wrong with doing something nice for yourself. Be selfish and do not feel guilty about it. Take solo trips. Treat yourself to dinner. Choose to show up for yourself. This inward realization of self-worth came while I was married. I concluded that my husband didn't love me for me. I didn't feel like he knew me well. That caused me to get angry and it caused a lot of conflict for us. So, I did something that changed my life. I created boundaries. Outside of setting boundaries, I allowed myself to authentically be me. That included having my hair a certain way or expressing how I feel.

My ultimate solitude and place of peace was in someone who was there all along. When I couldn't talk to anyone else, I could talk to God. If I had no place to go, I could go to God. If I didn't know which way to go, I could go through God. If no one else understood me, I knew God would understand me. God prepares me for now and He prepares me for whatever is next.

Next, for me, includes poetry and journaling in some form. My next includes the expansion of my personality and perspective. My life experiences were meant to be shared with young women. My grandmothers poured a great deal of life into me. When I think about their pour into me, I can only describe it as perseverance and pushing through. My maternal grandmother raised 13 children. My paternal grandmother raised five children. Both of my grandmothers were very dynamic. They both pushed through circumstances that were seemingly to their disadvantage. My grandmothers are a part of who I am today. They were God-fearing and they raised their families to know God and to have a relationship with God. They were also nurturers. They would feed you and everybody that came with you. There was always something on the stove cooking. Their home was open. If you needed a place to stay, come on in! In the homes of my grandparents, there was always a pour.

I want to pour in that same manner. I want to share with every woman that they all have a sense of beauty. Your beauty is uniquely yours. It doesn't have to look like anyone else's. It doesn't have to look like anyone else's journey. Your beauty and your journey are unique. Once you get past the surface level of who you are and what you know about yourself, you will discover, embrace and love yourself like never before. I believe that women are their most beautiful selves when they identify who she is as a queen.

Decema Wallace Pours

Email: decemasw33@gmail.com

My name is Decema. I am a young lady who is trying to tell her story. I'm understanding. I'm kind. The spirit of God has taught me how to extend grace to people. I believe that my story is part of my ministry. God has equipped me for this. Through trials and tribulations, I was stockpiling God's lessons. In my dark pit, I was learning. I have taken everything that God has given me and turned it into ministry. Once again, I am a young lady who is becoming a woman at the age of 43. Some of you may think that sounds strange. Your age does not make you an adult. At this point in my life, I am grateful to become the woman that I desire to be and the woman that God wants me to be. I've been experiencing a lot in my life. Some distractions. Some issues. Some weaknesses. Daily, God is identifying these things to me. As a young girl, I wanted to be loved. I wanted attention. I wanted to be seen. Even at the age of 43, I ask God to allow me to be seen and heard. Don't get me wrong. I'm not talking about someone seeing my body or my hair. I'm talking about my heart. Age doesn't mean anything. I'm growing in God because I want to be better. For me to be better, I have to have God. I tell people all the time – You may not need God, but you have to have Him. I can't live without God.

Here is some more insight into who I am. My mother was amazing. She raised seven kids as a single parent. To this day, she is the strongest woman that I have ever known outside of myself. My example of strength came from her. Her flaw was that she didn't know how to love. Love is who I am. Love is in my DNA, but love is what I was not getting. If God is love and He chose me from the womb, love is who I am.

I got saved in 2007 and I asked God for understanding. I couldn't understand how a mother could hate their child. A mother is supposed to love her child. Our childhood is a crucial moment in time. Our childhood is the time when the devil tries to kill us. The devil wants to kill us before we make it to purpose. He tries to kill our dreams. He tries to kill our desires. The devil tries to kill us before we become who we desire to be.

Without love, we are on a dark path that leads to nowhere. I grew up in the streets looking for love in all the wrong places. I had no emotions. I was always kind. I was always helping. I was always considerate of others. I knew no judgment, only love. I didn't see that growing up, but all of that had purpose. Everything we do has a purpose. Everything we say has a purpose. Every word we speak has a purpose. God doesn't waste anything.

As a young girl, I was doing drugs, and God spoke to me so clearly. Listen! God knows how to get your attention. I can remember it so clearly. I was in a hotel for three days getting high. God said to me, "If you don't stop snorting cocaine, you're going to be smoking crack". As much as I wanted to be seen, I was afraid to go down that road. On that third day, a Sunday, in 2007, I started going to church. I dove into church. I pleaded with God, "let me go to rehab. Please let me go to rehab." God said, "I am your rehab." From that day, I traveled this journey alone. No mother. No brother. No friend. I walked this journey alone. So, I have no choice but to let my journey be my ministry. Much like Joseph in the Bible, I experienced the pit. I want to encourage someone who may be reading my story. You are never so low that God's hand can't reach you. People talked about me. Yep! My family didn't believe in me. Yes and Yes again. I am a living testimony that you can do whatever you put your mind to with God. I wanted to give up. The burden of my life and it's assignment got very heavy. I told God, "I can't take it anymore." You have to listen to the spirit of God when He speaks and even more specifically when He provides instruction and direction. When I doubted myself, God said that He wouldn't have given it to me if He thought I couldn't handle it. Sometimes, you have to get out of yourself and out of your own way.

I don't do well with struggling. I watched my grandmother struggle in life. She was my mother. She raised me. I watched her go into the nursing home when I was 12-years-old. The enemy played so many tricks on my mind,. At one time, the enemy told me to kill myself. I said "No!". My children needed me. Then the enemy told me to kill them too. These were the strategic tricks of the enemty. The devil is very cunning. So, I was given the instructions to drive out in front of an 18-wheeler. But God! God said, don't do it. It won't work. I won't allow you to die even that way, but you will be in a bad situation if you be disobedient. Here we go again! I don't like to suffer and that would have been some suffering there. Even in my repeated cycles of hurt, disappointment, confusion, and brokenness, I chose God! Even as I am writin this chapter, I am being reminded that if God brought me out of those situations, He can bring me out of anything.

Through all of my hard times and situations, there was a lesson to be learned. My personal battles taught me how to be kind. They taught me how to be understanding.

My failures taught me to not judge. In my life, God is teaching me about grace.

Let me tell you about grace. I was on the phone with a good friend one day and the spirit of God moved on her to tell me that the same grace that God extends to me, He is expecting me to extend that same grace to my mother. That word dropped on me like a pile of bricks because I considered all of the things that I had done in my life and God forgave me. I thought about all of the times when God told me "No" and I said "Yes". I thought about all of the times when I ignored God and showed grace towards me. And now, I have to demonstrate that type of grace to my mother?!? Come on God! Are you serious? That's gonna be hard. When you stop and take accountability and assessment of your many negative deeds and actions, you will realize, it's not hard at all. When you walk in obedience, things have no choice but to line up. My journey has been hard, but it has made me better. I went back to school and got my bachelor's degree. I doubled my salary. I thought that I knew the ins and outs of this journey, but I am still learning and growing at the age of 43 and I've been in this for over 15 years.

If I could encourage someone at this moment, I would say to keep moving forward. In life, there will be moments when we have to stand still. That can be confusing. We don't understand it, but you have to have God. Healing comes from God. It's okay to be different. It's okay to be alone. It's okay to not be okay. Nothing about change is comfortable. Nothing about growth is comfortable. That's why they call them "growing pains".

If you fall down, get up, brush yourself off, get back in line, and start over. Every day, we have a choice and an opportunity to start over. What choice are you going to make today? How bad do you really want it? This isn't a fight where you have to use your hands, but you will need to use your knees. Fight in prayer and through prayer. That comes with a relationship with God. He's a God of grace. He' a God of forgiveness. He's a God of love. He's the God of my pour.

Alison Hill-Mitchell Pours

Alison Hill Mitchell
Instagram: @Alisonhillmitchell79
Facebook: Alison Hill Mitchell
Facebook: AHM Global Ministries
Email: ahmministries79@gmail.com

I'm going to let you know from the beginning that the pour you about to read is in a rough season. I'm pouring from a rough patch. I'm helping to lead a ministry. I'm a mother and now, a grandmother. I'm a wife. As soon as I accepted the assignment to pour in this anthology, my husband fell ill. I'm a songwriter and recording artist. I recently recorded a song called, "Take It To Jesus". The hook and drive of the song repeats, "He'll Fix It". I've needed the words of that song more than ever as I've been maneuvering through a burnout moment. I started working in New York at a daycare. Soon after that, I had hernia surgery. I had to decide if I was going to continue driving to New York. Traveling could be too much and cause hypothyroidism. That decision was on top of everything that I started with at the beginning of this chapter. I decided to get a job closer to home. At no time did I consider rest and recovery. Rightfully, I should have taken four to six weeks to recover, but at the three-week mark, I was back at work. My family reminded me that ministry was a full-time job for me. It had already been prophesied that ministry will take care of me, but when my husband got ill and stopped working, I took on a full-time job to help make ends meet.

All I know is how to make things happen. My family cannot lack. At that time, I had a 14-year-old in high school as a freshman. I had a daughter who was trying to get on her feet with a newborn baby and they all live with me. Recently, my husband and I spoke to our family. They saw me in a weak, burnout, vulnerable moment. Most of the time, they rely on me in their moment, but the roles were reversed. I'm one of 11 children, but you would think that I was the oldest. I'm actually the 4th of the 11 children. I was the first to get married. I was the first to have a child. I have the longest marriage as compared to my siblings. My daughter was the first grand and now we've given my mother her first great-grandchild. In ministry, my pastor is 74 years old and she is grooming me to be her assistant. My ministerial journey is a roller coaster in and of itself. In a nutshell, I have experienced temporary seasons for a permanent. I've dealt with church hurt and issues. I am a witness that God will cause chaos in the midst of a situation just to get you to move. I was part of a church where the leader of the church didn't consider me to be a leader, when in actuality, all I did was lead. During the pandemic, I led all of the virtual services and prayer calls. God told me to shift and I didn't listen. God moved me from that situation and I did praise and worship for different churches. One Sunday, a friend of mine did a solo just to give us a break. I went to the restroom and cried. God reminded me that this was just a temporary situation and to do it scared. That same day, I had a rehearsal and a friend of mine was used by God to remind me, once again, that this was only temporary and to do it scared. He went on to say that there are some unfamiliar people that God is preparing me to lead. Two weeks after that, I got a call from the woman who is now my pastor, saying I need help. She needed assistance in praise and worship. After a very detailed conversation, God told me to be there for her. I've been there for two years now. Since being there, I have been elevated to Evangelist and now, I am being prepared for another elevation that will allow me to operate in more of an Assistant Pastor role. One of our members who served as my armorbearer passed away in a tragic car accident. One day, she didn't show up to church and we were later notified of her transition. Due to how close my Pastor was to this young lady, it was too hard for her to stand in that capacity. She passed the baton to me and I ended up officiating that homegoing. God has equipped me and placed me in positions that I didn't think I was ready. After that, I sang a song for a co-worker at his repast and ended up doing somewhat of a memorial for him. All of this is going on and transpiring in my life leading up to one of the biggest and hardest hitting events in my life with the killing of my baby brother.

My brother was standing in a complex parking lot. Some guys had a disagreement over a dice game, exchanged gun fire, and hit my brother in the head. Now, I stand proxy for my family on Zoom calls during the hearings. After I've been strength for so many other families, I now have to be strength for my family as a representative and it's only by the grace of God.

It's only by the grace of God that I am able to pour. I'm not a SuperWoman, but I am God's woman. When you're God's woman, He will give you everything you need to get everything done. You're wondering where that strength comes from and it comes from God. You're wondering how you accomplished that and it was a God thing. You're wondering why people are drawn to you and it's because you were chosen by God.

My family values run deep. First and foremost, my family is rooted in and built on love. Actually, I would say love and determination are strong family values. I never saw my parents struggle. They didn't put that on display. Now, if the lights got turned off, they would turn that into some type of fun activity. We never knew our lights were out. We just had fun and my dad would have the lights turned on the next morning. They showed us that they had the determination to push through any situation. Out of all of my mother's children, I exemplify determination. If I'm going through, I'm not going to say much. I'm just going to pray through it and say that I believe God. A lot of people use the acronym LOL for Laugh Out Loud. Well, I believe in speaking VOL, meaning Victory Out Loud. Our friends wonder "how do you get through what you go through?" and "how do you get through obstacles, trials and tribulations?".

The beginning of my marriage was a challenge. We were separated for five years. My husband did not know how to love and when he entered in our new space of marriage, it was a strange land for him. I don't think he knew what true love was. At the beginning of our marriage, he was abusive. He didn't know why, but he later learned that generation curses are real. His dad took him away from his family at an early age. During our separation, he met his biological mother. Everything happens for a reason. We got married at a very young home. I came from a loving home.

I was loved the way a young lady should be loved. I never saw my parents argue. If they did, we never heard them. I was groomed into love. I was groomed into determination.

My determination and example of love reaches to people that are not the typical church. One time, I participated in a talent showcase at the Cole Brightside Tavern. As much as I wanted to do some Lauryn Hill song or something similar, the curator wanted me to do some gospel. Because of the light that God has planted inside of me, I have been invited back multiple times. I had to preach a few Sundays after being at the showcase and some of the young ladies from Brightside came to church that Sunday. I am reminded of the prophetic word that was spoken over my life that I would be called to unfamiliar places to lead unfamiliar people. My example of determination was demonstrated to me at an early age. My dad would take me everywhere with him to see how things went with elevations and I never understood why. He was grooming me. When it was time for me to be elevated, my Overseer told me that I wasn't doing this from scratch. I was starting from experience. I've been ministering. I've been helping everybody's church. I've been helping everybody's outreach. I've been supporting everybody. That's what has made me a strong leader and preacher. My dad was very pivotal in that and my parents guided me in love and wisdom.

Yolanda Harris Pours

Email: yolaharr@aol.com

My name is Yolanda Harris. I'm a single mother. I'm an entrepreneur and philanthropist. I have a nonprofit organization called Hearts That Care of South Carolina. We serve the homeless community around the state. We also serve the foster children in Sumter, South Carolina. I'm a licensed property manager. I have my license to be a property manager in charge and property management to sell them. While in college, I was in the computer lab filling out applications and I received a phone call. This lady offered me a part-time job in property management. Two weeks into this job, I thought it wasn't for me. I made up my mind to go to lunch and not go back. She refused to accept my resignation. I had such an attitude. After an hour, I went back to work. Do you know that April will be ten years for me in the property management industry? On top of that, I am an author. That started with a journal. I'm also a notary public for Richland County in the state of South Carolina. I wear so many hats. Everything I do is to serve. I just want God to use me in my community, in my family, in my church and in my career. The bizarre thing is that all of these opportunities fell into my lap. I didn't go searching for any of it. It was sent to me by God.

My inspiration to keep going and to find new ways to serve is my faith and my faith in God. Life has a way of sending obstacles and challenges. Times really get hard and seemingly cause you to say, "I'm not going to do this anymore." There are times when we want to bail out or walk away. However, when you are walking in purpose, on purpose, it does not matter how much or how often you want to quit. He won't let you. He's going to keep pushing you. He has an endless supply of energy to provide to you to keep going. He will also send people, places, and things your way to remind you about why you're doing what you're doing. That's what He does for me and to me.

Recently, I was impressed with the concept that it costs nothing to be kind. When you are kind to people, people will do unexpected things for you. Doors of opportunities will be open to you. It's like the favor of God is on your life and there isn't a thing that you can do about it. I tell people all the time, I am a servant. Above every title, position and accolade, I am a servant. I just want to serve well.

My "Why" is my family. I started Hearts That Care based on circumstances that were going on in my life. As many people say, "life wasn't life-ing". I was in a struggle, but I had a heart for the homeless. My dad died on the couch in a local homeless shelter in 1998. To see what he went through and how it was handled, pulled on my heartstrings. I believe that God allowed me to go through things just to give me a glimpse of what he went through. My inspiration can be found in a lot of people. My family inspires me. My bonus family pushes me. My pastor's wife, Dr. Peggy Johnson encourages me. My children. My dad. My mom. My coach, K. I have 10 god-children and a roster of bonus babies. I've been privileged to see them become entrepreneurs and community leaders. That lets me know that I'm doing something right. That also lets me know that they are always watching. When people watch you or see you, what are you putting on display?

Let's talk about my life's journey that all of these people inspire. This journey is not easy. Being a philanthropist and an entrepreneur is not for the weak. You come in contact with people who don't want to support you. You meet people who don't want to give. There are times when you have to come out of pocket. Coach K instructed me about my job being my biggest investor. I told God years ago that I didn't want a non-profit. How does God want me to product a service for people that I need myself? How can I give from what I don't have? When I look back over my life, everything that I needed, God provided. When I needed food to feed my children, someone would call with loads of food. Then, I wanted to go back to school, but I wasn't working. At that time, I hadn't worked since 2006 because I was sick. God told me to go back to school. Come on God! I don't even have the gas to put in my van to get me back and forth to school. He made a way every time!

I started telling God everything. Lord, I need income! One day at South University they were having Student Appreciation Day. I was walking by the Financial Aid Office and Mr. Rickey started walking with me as I was going to get something to eat. In casual conversation, he asked, "Are you still looking for a work-study job?"

I said, "Yes, why?"

He replied, "One just came available. When can you start? Come to my office after your class so we can fill out the paperwork and set your schedule."

I was sitting there like, "God, I just told you that I needed income and you came through immediately!" It wasn't a lot, but it was just what I needed. After doing that job for about a year and a half, the Assistant Dean of Student Affairs asked me to come to her office. I was scared because I thought I did something wrong. She informed me that the work-study job was coming to an end. Immediately, I was clueless as it related to my next step. What am I going to do? She mentioned that although my current position was coming to an end, they already had a plan to hire me in Student Affairs, making more money.

Here's how God does it for me – Before I can pray about a thing, God already works out the details. That takes me back to my faith. Doors that I don't even know about are being opened for me.

My assignment and mission is to serve God and to do His will. During that process, I am fighting through some excruciating pain. I have a cane, but I refuse to use when I'm not at home because it slows me down. My focus is not on the pain. I can rest when I get home. If I need to sit down or lie down, I can. If I looked at the pain or the swelling, I wouldn't get anything done. In my mind, if don't do anything, I failed God. In 2006, I died on the operating table. I was in ICU for a month. When they brought me back, I had a trach and a colostomy. I questioned God as to why he brought me back. My kids could have lived off of my social security and insurance. Did God bring me back to suffer and struggle? God reminded me that He brought me back because I still had work to do. So, I can never concentrate on the pain. The moment I give energy to my pain, I take the strength away from my purpose. When I speak life to my pain, I kill my vision. I have a lot of work to do. I'm in the full-time blessing business. I want to bless people with cars, houses and food. I want to sow into the lives of people anonymously. I can't do that if I keep feeling sorry for myself. My Pastor taught me that if I take care of God's people, He will take care of me. Daily he proves Himself to me. Every day. Every step. He has never let me down.

If I could leave anything with you in this chapter, I would encourage you to trust God. When I started, I didn't know anything. I was an empty vessel and a clean slate. God spoke. I listened and I moved. It's not always going to be easy, but God will send the right people to help you. Keep going. Do your research. Study. Be persistent. Be intentional. God is going to provide for you and he is going to take care of you.

Ryann CoachRah Carter Pours

Website: www.PursuitOfYourPurposeLLC.org

Facebook: Pursuit of your Purpose LLC

Email: PursuitOfYourPurpose@gmail.com

My name is Ryann Carter. I am an overcomer. I don't prefer the term survivor. When you are an overcomer, the things that tried to hold you back no longer have you in bondage. I am a mother, a friend, a daughter. I'm a godmother. I'm an aunt. I'm everything to everyone but I'm also something to myself. I am my own identity. I am my own piece of hope. I am my own empowerment because of everything that I have gone through.

My pour for women comes from my roots. My journey starts from my childhood. I'm pretty sure I met my daddy earlier, but my earliest recollection of him was when I was six years old. He passed when I was 14. I experienced daddy issues and abandonment for a long time from a man who repeatedly broke promises. I tried to build a relationship with an absent daddy. I was almost 30 years old when I made some strides towards forgiveness. I went through a marriage that was verbally, physically, and mentally abusive. It pulled me away from my friends because I was with a man in whom I sought the validation that I never received as a child. He took everything from me. In a back-and-forth battle for years, I fought to regain stability and my identity. I believe that I made about 90% progress when I realized that I wanted to empower women. If you truly want to know what your purpose is, find your passion. My passion is to see others well and healed. I've always been the type of person who wanted to make other people happy even when I was going through my own battles. I was pouring, but I was empty. I was going through abuse, and no one knew it. I chose to show up for everybody else. My goal was to empower everyone, but I was forgetting about myself. I believe that I had to go through, what I call, chapters of life so someone else would know how to overcome the same obstacles. In my marriage, I was blocked from so much including the achievement of my degree. When I finally earned my Associate's degree, it was a major accomplishment because it took me eight years to get it. That allows me to tell my daughter that I went through so you don't have to go through.

I pour because I understand the struggle. I understand the silent frustrations. I understand what it is to not have anyone to listen to you when you have made a choice to kill yourself. I want to be the open-door policy person. I'm not here to judge. I know how it feels to be alone. I know what it feels like when no one understands. I want to be the resource that people can lean on. This is why I am here.

The driving forces to my pour are my mother and my daughter. I watched a mother raise three children by herself while working a full-time job. My daughter is my everything and I want to make sure I show up for her. I can remember on her first day of school in public school. She had an event and I was determined to be there. I called in late to work to make sure I was there for my daughter. One of the kids at the school was looking for his mother and I felt bad for him because I remembered not having my mother at every event. She couldn't be there. She has three kids and a mortgage and she had to make things happen. My situation is different. I'll get paid on my day off so I'm going to be there for my daughter. My motivation and my inspiration are in seeing the smile on my daughter's face. Everything that I do in life are for my mother and my daughter. My daughter doesn't have to grow up in the trauma that I wasn't healed from. I'm able to allow her to live a healthy and whole life.

The challenges of my life included low self-esteem. I didn't see myself as being valuable. I was always looking for validation. I didn't know what love was. In my warped reality, if he didn't hit me, he didn't love me. If he didn't talk bad about me, he didn't love me. I had so many insecurities. I was told "you're pretty, but you're big" or "you're ugly". In marriage, I was told "you'll never going to be good enough" and "you'll never be a mother". I struggled with low self-esteem for years. I tried my best to fit in. I cut my hair. I colored my hair. I straightened my hair. It didn't matter what I did. I could never fit in. Then, I had this experience where I was placed in front of a mirror for a moment of reflection. I had to talk to myself. That thing broke me. I realized that I was beautiful. I was intelligent. I was smart. I was loved.

All purpose is for something. I believe that someone is waiting for me to align with them. If I'm out of position or not doing something that I'm supposed to be doing, I'm holding someone else up. If I'm not operating in my purpose, I am preventing the breakthrough of someone else. Daily, I remind myself to be in place. If there's a need, I have to fulfill it. Whether it's a hug or a support system, I have to show up. If I decline the need, I fail the person. It's almost like a relay race. I can't choose to stop in the middle of the race. If I do, the next person will not be able to move. It's a domino effect. Even if I don't feel like doing it, I have to do it. I'm called to it. From the beginning of time, God created your purpose. If I walk in my purpose, the next person can win. If they win, the person connected to their win, wins. We can't afford to miss opportunity. It's like entertaining angels. Recently, I was at the doctor's office having casual conversation in the lobby with a lady and I said, "you look good". She said that she needed to hear that. If I had canceled my appointment, I would have missed an opportunity to empower someone.

There is a story about a rose that grows from concrete. Not many people notice if the rose is battered or bruised. They are mainly intrigued because it is growing from a hard place. They are surprised that it is blooming from an unexpected situation. That's how your life is set up. Regardless of what is going on around you and regardless of your circumstances, you have an opportunity to bloom right where you are planted. As humans, we are going to have our days. The key to success is that we can't allow our days to have us. Even in your pouring, don't forget to pour into yourself. Make yourself a priority.

Menia "LadyRedd" Lockhart Pours

Email: Ladyreddevents@gmail.com

I am Lady Red Lockhart and my Yes is very synonymous with what I have going on right now that's in the pipeline. A few years ago, God gave me a movement called Life After Divorce and Death: Learning How To Live and Love Again. It's a personal story and testament of my life. I was married for nine years before getting a divorce. A year later, my former husband was killed in a car accident with the woman he was involved with before our divorce was final. Both of them died. It was really tragic. After a couple of years, I moved home to care for my mother, Christina Johnson Bryce, until her demise and God birthed Life After Divorce and Death. Immediately, God told me that I was going to help women.

Initially, my primary focus was women, but after hosting a very small and intimate event, a couple of men reached out to tell me that my vision was not just for women. Some men had been divorced multiple times and were struggling with living and loving after the divorce. One of things that changed my business approach was when I included therapists as my conference vendors. I wasn't looking for t-shirt, soap and jewelry vendors. I needed therapists, mental health clinicians, and licensed practical counselors. My therapist availed herself immediately. I reached out to people that were part of my healing journey. I went back to the drawing board. I started over and this time, it was bigger. It was global.

I knew that participating in this She Pours Collaboration would allow me to share with more women. It was prophesied to me about writing a book and this opportunity fulfilled it. Now, I'm working on a healing journal.

I experienced my own Life After Divorce and Death. I got divorced. I was trying to get back to myself and then he died. So, I was back to grieving and spiraled into depression and anger. I was a single mother on top of taking care of my mother. Then, she transitioned and there was more grief. This Life After movement is ongoing. Not only are people dealing with life after divorce and death, but they are also dealing with life after this, life after abuse, life after infidelity, life after homosexuality, life after being married to a narcissist, life after being in an unfulfilled relationship, life after a miscarriage, and the list also goes on and on. Everything that I do is birthed from experience.

My marriage experience is a major part of my journey. I always desired to be married. My mother always taught me to go to college, make something of myself and get my own husband, not someone elses, my own. So I did just that. I graduated high school, graduated from two colleges, moved to Charlotte and this man found me. I got married because I loved him. I didn't want to play house. I wanted to get married. Both of our families were divorce-stricken. We didn't have an example of a healthy marriage. All we knew was that we loved each other. We wanted a healthy marriage and we tried. I did the best that I could to keep the marriage intact. However, it didn't last. The marriage failed due to lack of communication and disrespect. Our marriage failed because he didn't want it anymore. There were times when I was verbally and physically abusive. This came as a result of my insecurities and a lack of self-control. He told me that if I hit him again, he would leave. I didn't listen and I took him for granted. When I finally got myself together, it was too late. The God-fearing woman who loved Jesus that he fell in love with came back too late. He had on blinders to my change for the better. I accepted my role in our divorce. I pushed him away. I actually pushed him into the arms of another woman. One day, we had a real heart-to-heart, and I apologized for my wrongdoings. I apologized for hurting him. I apologized for being selfish. All of that was part of my healing. At the beginning of our divorce, it was hard because he wasn't helping with our son or spending quality time with him. Then, he got a new job and inquired about putting our son on his insurance and paying a certain amount for support each month. We agreed on that. One day, while driving to Augusta, he called just to check on us. At the end of our conversation, we simply said that we would talk to each other later, but later never came.

Some of the characteristics that inspire me are strength, faith, courage, and wisdom. So many people look up to me. My siblings, my nieces, my nephews, and my friends. They are always pulling on me. I've always known that I had the gift to motivate, encourage, and inspire. I knew that one day, my gifts would make room for me. I went to a lot of conferences and church events and had many people to pour life into me. I made up my mind to hold on to the word of God. I reminded God of His word and that I wasn't going through this for nothing. God chose me for such a time as this. Now, I'm no longer living in the pain. Now, I'm on the other side. I'm living the promise. I'm turning the pain into purpose. I didn't think I was going to make it out, but I did.

God chose me for this. He didn't want me to be a widower. My former husband left me in 2014. Throughout 2015, I prayed. I travailed. I fasted. Then, in 2016, on GroundHog Day, I woke up and God instructed me to go downtown and file the paperwork. I took my son to the daycare and went downtown to start the process. It took a year and a half. One weekend, he came home for the weekend and I told him to meet me at the bank. He had no idea what was going on, but the final step was to sign the paperwork in front of a notary public. We experienced some rough patches when the divorce was final, but life came back around full circle. I wasn't going to answer the phone that day when I was driving to Augusta. I actually laughed when the call came through like, "what does this man want?". I answered the call and we talked briefly. Needless to say, I will never forget August 9th, 2017. That was the last time we communicated.

My goal and continual prayer is to operate in purposeful time. I have a job as an ABA therapist and I love working with preschoolers with autism. I'm in no rush to quit my job. My therapist encourages me by saying, "Work your 9-5 until your passion can pay for your lifestyle."

I'm on the road to that. I desire to operate full-time with my weddings and empowerment experiences. I don't prefer to use the term conference because that makes me feel like someone is going to lecture to me all day.

I choose empowerment experiences because I like to create environments where you will experience empowerment. Daily, I strive for purpose over popularity.

TANYA MOORE POURS

Facebook: Tanya Moore
Instagram: @ Pastor_ma
Instagram: @kehah counseling

Let me start by saying that my yes to participate in this anthology came after I attended the premiere of the film, She Pours. I thought it was phenomenal. As the women in the film shared their points of view, it inspired me to see how, and what they poured. Most women can see themselves in any of the portrayed situations. When I heard about this opportunity, it was a no-brainer.

Now that the preliminaries are out of the way, my name is Tanya Moore, and I was born and raised in Harlem, New York. I am so grateful for is that I did not become a statistic. I grew up in a female-dominated household and was the product of alcoholic parents. There was no male influence after the age of nine when my grandfather died.

My father was not in my life (As an adult I found out that he lived three blocks down from us, with his wife and my half-brother). My mother was a mean drunk, and my maternal grandmother was my protector until the day she died. She found herself in the crossfire of some violent arguments; my mother would knock her to the floor, but she was my buffer. My grandmother loved me unconditionally and instilled morals and values in my young life. Her Social Security kept the household going; while she raised and nurtured me to adulthood. When my grandmother died, I left the house before my mother and I killed each other. I was tired of being her punching bag. Alcohol took my mother's life at the age of 43 due to alcoholism, hypertension and renal failure. My father did not fare much better; he died at age 50 from alcohol, diabetes and a heart attack. The statistics declare that I should be an alcoholic, but God. I moved to Albany, NY and met my husband, joined the United States Air Force, and we started our family. I had jumped out of the fire and into the frying pan, my husband also became an alcoholic. My marriage and raising our children was challenging, although there were some good times. Once I retired from the Air Force after 20 years, I went back to school in my late 40's. I earned my bachelor's and a Master of Divinity in Pastoral Counseling. In the midst of school, my husband died. I felt he was taken too soon but God knew best. And oh by the way, the Lord also told me to birth a church, Fallow Ground Ministries.

My pour can be illustrated from many positions. From growing up in an abusive home, serving in the military, losing my husband, and pastoring a church. Then, I realized later in life that I was an addiction enabler. My God-given purpose is a healer. As women, we are nurturers and want to fix everything. We want to make things right. We want to fix them. We want to change them. Here's an early lesson that many women don't learn in relationships and marriages: you can't change that person. But we do have the power to choose. Can we live with it? Is this a deal breaker? God is the only One Who can change a person.

Growing up in a household of women, I became a control freak. In my marriage I was the breadwinner, and made sure the bills were paid. I did not have a pattern for marriage. I didn't know how a wife should speak to her husband. Women want to be loved and have a sense of security. Men want to be loved and respected. I crossed that line with my husband many times until the Holy Ghost told me to be quiet. You don't have to engage in every disagreement. You don't have to win every argument. And when you argue with someone who is addicted, you are the fool. You are sober and their mind is altered. When I learned that, the arguments were less frequent and short-lived.

I am transitioning from grieving to thriving, and I'm living on the other side of grief. I want to get married again. I want a man that understands my ministry and the gift that God has placed in my life, I believe God will send me someone who I can walk side-by-side with and do the work of the Lord. That is my next. I want to offer some nuggets of wisdom and possibly save someone the heartache that I experienced. I have connected with a wonderful ministry. Our mandate is to reclaim families, who in turn will heal communities. Our reach is inside and outside of the four walls. We are gap fillers. If there is a need, we seek to fill it.

I have three wonderful children: two daughters and one son, and eight grandchildren. As a Pastor, I would like to encourage everyone to have a relationship with God. That is where you draw your strength to pour. Oftentimes, we pour and pour and fail to replenish. You can't pour from an empty cup. Take time for self-care. Take a moment to get your feet done. Take time to do absolutely nothing. You have to re-energize and stay connected to the source, and that source is God.

Imani Peterkin Pours

Email: imaniwilsonpeterkin@gmail.com

My name is Imani Wilson Peterkin. I gave my "Yes" to this project because I believe that someone's freedom is tied to it. My "Yes" to this project is connected to my obedience to do what God has called me to. Lastly, my "Yes" was easily submitted based on the credibility of the visionary and the create a safe place for sharing and pouring. This is why I am sharing my story.

I am from Columbia, South Carolina. I was born and raised there and never lived anywhere else. I lived in a single-parent home, but we moved around a lot. When I say a lot, I really A LOT! We moved almost every school year. I like to joke about it, but I've been in every school district in Columbia. This was mainly due to finances, so it made growing up very unstable. As soon as we got comfortable, we had to start over. We struggled a lot. It got even worse in high school because my mother was diagnosed with lupus. That flipped our world upside down. After that, we had to move in with family. I thought that was a good thing for us. We moved in with my grandmother. My grandmother was a God-fearing woman. If you live in her house, you're going to church every Sunday. Every Sunday!

In my childhood, from the age of 13 to my early 20's, I suffered with depression. That's not something that I haven't shared too often, but I think it is very important. My mother did the best that she could with what she had. All of my childhood experiences contributed to what I am doing now. It led me to create a non-profit organization that helps underserved communities. I know what it's like to go without. I know what it is to now know where your next meal is coming from. That's where my passion is driven, especially for little black girls. I pride myself on being a first generation college student. It was not easy, but it was possible. I'm in school now and it's not easy, but it's possible. I want to show little girls that it's possible.

I graduated from Irmo High School and then graduated from Strayer University. This part of my life was a journey. As I said, I was a first-generation college student. Initially, I went to Bennett College in North Carolina. This was about four hours away and everything was fine. They offered me a scholarship, but when I arrived, it was revoked for some reason that we still haven't figured out to this day. I was there for about a month in hopes of setting up a payment plan for the remaining balance. Well, I couldn't make the payments and my access to my dorm and the cafeteria was cut off. Here I am. Four hours from home. No family nearby. I couldn't get into my dorm. I couldn't get into the cafeteria for food. Did that stop me? No! For a period of time, I had some friends prop the door open so I could get into my dorm if I had to leave. Ultimately, my parents came and got me. In a sense, I felt defeated, but I was trying to stay determined. So, I went to Strayer. I was there for a little while before my friend convinced me to go to Lander. It was a good experience, but I had too much freedom. That amount of freedom became a distraction and I flunked out.

My mental state was not in a good place and I resorted to drinking. That was not good based on my family history. So, I ended back at home..... again. Then, my life really changed when I found out that I was pregnant with my daughter. That changed the trajectory of my life. I was having a kid. My job was only paying $10 per hour. I didn't have a car. I had to do something and quick! I had responsibilities. I went back to school and got my Associate's degree. A year later, I finished my Bachelor's degree and now, I'm on my journey to complete my doctorate.

I would attribute the inspiration of all of my life's accomplishments to my daughter. I've always known that she depends on me. Even though she was a baby, I always wanted to provide a better life for her. Not only for her, but also for myself. I didn't grow up in the best situation. My mother didn't go to college. She did the best that she could with what she had. I knew that if I went to school, doors of opportunity would open for me. I believe that anything that I do is bigger than me especially if God led me to do it. That's why I had to keep going. I show up to show other girls that they can do it too. That's one of my mottos in life. It's always bigger than me even if I don't understand it in the moment.

Getting pregnant with my daughter was a gift from a traumatic situation. I went to a party with, who I thought was a friend. I was in a place that I wasn't familiar with. I didn't have a car. I was drinking and ended up getting drugged. That's the foundation of the traumatic situation. Another layer to that situation was that the person I went to the party with was the culprit behind the entire ordeal. I haven't shared this information much but I believe that releasing this information is part of the healing process. I'm learning to share my story. In times past, I've been the strong person and proclaimed that stuff will never happen to me. I learned that you can never say never because you never know what can happen.

On the other side of this ordeal, I am healing and building my relationship with God. That's the only thing that keeps me on track. Talking about that situation was an open wound that revealed other issues that I needed to be healed from. My healing process was different. My dad is a Pastor. Yes! I'm a preacher's kid. My healing journey started with fasting and prayer. I also journaled a lot and allowed myself to feel my feelings. When you are going through your healing process, you must be real with yourself. You have to dig deep into the root and cause of your feelings. Why does that trigger? Why does that make me feel the way it does? This is what I had to do to heal.

This is what positioned me to do what I do. I want to change the lives of young girls and women. My organization is called Brown Girls of Tomorrow. The idea of this organization comes from a comical beginning. Remember, God is always intentional. You can never run from the call. Brown Girls of Tomorrow didn't happen by happenstance. Brown Girls of Tomorrow was birthed during my time at Lander. I was gleaning ideas from another non-profit. I didn't think that I was a good example. During the pandemic, God reminded me of the vision. I was in a better place. My fiancé at the time, who is now my husband, told me to just do it. Self-sabotage tried to sneak in. Skepticism tried to rise up. Doubt tried to manifest. I knew I had to trust God. He qualified me before I knew it. I went through the business creation process and got everything I needed to make it happen. The program is based on need, and it started in 29203, a zip code and area of Columbia, South Carolina. That is so significant for me. I had to start at Hyatt Park. That's where my story started before I was even born. My parents grew up there. My grandmother ran a daycae there for over 20 years off Farrow Road. My grandparents are still homeowners in the area. I had to bring it back home. That's where I spent part of my childhood. I needed to impact the lives of girls in that community. Young girls from that area are turned away. They are looked upon as adults and not children. I brought it back home and it has been history in the making ever since. In 2024, we are celebrating four years of existence and this has been one of our greatest years of operation.

We offer mentors, workshops, mental health awareness programs, college readiness and financial literacy. One of our main events was previously called Motivational Saturdays, but we have turned it into Power Her Spark Conference. The purpose of this event is to pour into our youth before they go back to school. We have keynote speakers that come in and speak to the youth. The best thing is that it's not just for the youth. It's the adults too. We have Parent Table Talk where the parents have a private session to discuss their concerns and needs. We want to pour into the parents so they can be equipped to be better parents. We connect the families to community resources. It really takes a village. I'm excited for what God is doing through the organization and I can't wait to see what He does next. I'm not going to lie. When faced with this great vision, it takes me out of my comfort zone, but I always remind myself, it's bigger than me.

Tina Darlene Torres Pours

Website: www.shedidthatevents.com
Instagram: @shedidthateventsllc
Facebook: tinadarlenetorres
Email: tinatorres@shedidthatevent.com

My name is Tina Darlene Torres. My service to others is based on the trauma that I experienced in life as a child. I've always wanted people not to feel disregarded, hurt, blindsided, misused or abused. These are all things that I experienced as I was growing up. I have always sought out ways and methods to make sure somebody had something to eat or clothes on their back. When I got my first home in 1997, it wasn't my home because I always let people stay here. My life of service and my give back are embedded in me because of trauma. I want to be a resource. If you call Tina, she is going to have an answer. That has been my life since 1996/1997. At that time, I was around 24 or 25 years old with three small children under the age of 7. It may have kicked in before that, but I didn't notice it. This is my thing. This is my niche. Always available. Always present. Always positioned to help someone that is in need of assistance.

My pour is not maintained. Let me explain that. Serving, for me, is mandatory. It's an everyday occurrence. Serving is my internal and external contribution in the earth. I don't think a day goes by without me verbalizing, "Are you good?", "Are you okay?", and "Do you need anything?". It's so natural for me and it happens daily. To me, it's as consistent as brushing your teeth, washing your face, and putting on the proper clothing for the day. It's never rehearsed. It's not forced. It is something that is naturally there. That's what I prepare for. Daily, I put my game face on and my game face says, "I'm here for you!"

In terms of service, my life's work is scaling back some. The older I get, the more secluded and protective of myself I become. I believe it is time for the next generation of servants to come forward with their creativity and innovative methods to help those in need. In this next phase of my life, I want to be able to enjoy life. I recently received a full scholarship to Midlands Technical College for their continuing education program to become a Patient Care Technician. I will still be working with people, but the resources will be more accessible. Instead of walking up to the front door, only to be told "No", I'll be coming in the back door where I can get my hands on the resources a little easier to serve the needs of the community.

My leadership prowess has been catapulted in a different direction. For many years, I was the Olivia Pope. I just want to enjoy whatever time I have left. I don't know what tomorrow is going to bring or the day after that. I don't have to be in the driver's seat anymore. I don't have to be the leader. More recently, I have been comfortable with working behind the scenes. I'm really good at delegating and helping others to be seen. Nowadays, I'm not out everywhere as people are more accustomed to. I'm learning how to use my time more wisely. Being everywhere for everyone was killing me internally, mentally, physically, spiritually, and financially. That said, if I choose to be a leader in anything, it's going to be to create a legacy for my kids. Truth be told, I don't even have to be in a leadership position to do that.

My commitments are shifting too. I just want to get pretty and attend an event without working. Tina, can you do this? No. I'm an attendee. I am committed to doing something for me. If that means pulling back, I'm ok with that. If that mean losing people, places and all the things, I'm ok. This new shift in my life comes with a renewed commitment to let go. My definition of loyalty was warped. My loyalty meant that I had to work with "them". Loyalty meant that I had to collaborate with "them" because of who they are. That mentality got me no where. I don't have to be with the loudest group on social media. I don't have to be in the loudest group on the front line. My volume on social media has lessened. No longer am I conforming to what people want me to be. I have had too many suicidal thoughts because of the expectations and opinions of people. I have to let go. Receiving this scholarship to go back to school was God's way of saying, I'm moving you in a different direction and I need you to pay attention. I have student loans that are in default. You're not supposed to get that scholarship if your loans are in default. I got the scholarship!

My life of service has been great, but this new season that I am in is causing me to look out for myself more. It is imperative that you seek out the assistance to make things happen. Tough times don't always last, but if you just sit back, you will make the time last longer than necessary. We can't afford to sit around and expect things to come to us. It doesn't work like that. If you want a different outcome, you have to do something different. You have to seek it. Figure it out. Google it. Read about it. Outline it. Map it out. Put a timeline on it. Execute it. My life has been such a roller coaster that I forgot that it was okay to just coast. When you coast, you have put in enough work (speed) to coast. When you coast, you can smell the flowers. You can see the rainbows. You can watch the clouds form. You can do all of that and not feel guilty about it.

There is so much more to life than being in the "in crowd." The "in crowd" is not the place to be. That's where they have pity parties. They gather to have pity talks and boost their pitiful egos to be even more mean and more rude to others. I'm ok with not being in the "in crowd." It wasn't built for me.

Times have changed so much. I love people and that's never going to change. Even when people have done me wrong, I still loved them. I also knew how to act accordingly. I am shifting to doing more for me. Serving is not like a ball and chain unless you make it that way by not setting boundaries. When you don't set boundaries, you will get burned out. I was burned out and it was no one's fault but my own. It's time to pass the torch to the next generation that is looking for ways to assist people who are in need. I'm always going to be here, but it's time for a change. It's time for something new and something different. I'm a military brat. I know change. I know how to adapt. I'm accustomed to traveling and learning new things. I don't want to be boxed into the Olivia Pope persona when there are more and better things that I can do. There are so many ways to do life and so many classes, training, and opportunities out there. That's how I got the scholarship and got back into school. It is an opportunity, and I got it! I want people to create boundaries, live life, and go for what they want.

It's pretty dope to leave a legacy. It's the best thing. I may not be rich in favor, but I am rich in love, rich in passion, and rich in God's eyes. That's all that matters to me.

Nina Jetana Rogers Pours

Email: ninajetana@yahoo.com

My name is Nina Jetana Rogers. God has always instructed me that if I pour from my testimony through the storms of life, He will continue blessing me to be able to pour. I have come a long way in life. I'm the oldest of all of my siblings. I don't feel like I had a childhood. I experienced a lot of neglect and abuse in different ways. I know what it is like to be depressed. I know what it is to experience anxiety. In the midst of my own personal storm, I had to pick myself up. My advice to myself was that if I wanted to fill someone else's cup, I had to allow God to fill mine. I had to go through everything that I've been through so I could help others. I am grateful that I don't look like what I've been through.

I am from Bennetsville, South Carolina in Marlboro County around the Pee Dee/Florence area. I'm a city and country girl! Growing up, I always wanted to be a teacher. Entering into my junior year at Benedict College, my career goals. I didn't want to be a teacher anymore, but I wanted to be a counselor. I wanted to help people. That also came from what I experienced as a child and teenager. I've noticed that a lot of cities lack resources to help people. I don't just counsel you. I network with others. That way, if I don't have the tool or resource, I can direct you to the person who does.

My pour is inspired by multiple people. My mom is a very strong person. My baby sister inspires me. My Godfather inspires me. And Kiwan inspires. I can remember having so many conversations when I felt like I was at my lowest and God will guide my footsteps to one of these individuals to get what I needed to tackle any and all assignments. God always gives them the right words to say.

After they have poured into me, I am better equipped to pour into others. Opportunities to pour find me with ease. My phone is always ringing and my messenger stays loaded with calls and messages for help. Sometimes they need encouragements. Sometimes they need an escape. The people that I come in contact with are going through so much from depression to domestic violence to physical and mental abuse. I have to position myself to fulfill needs at all times. Most of what they are going through, I have been through. My example of going through the process and coming out on the other side is influential and instrumental in their success and forward progress. My communications start vague with the "Hey! How are you doing?" In most cases, I can feel and sense that this person needs something. It could be to just vent or it can be a slight smoke signal. Needless to say, I make myself available to pour and serve. At the end of it all, the person just wanted to be heard. They don't want to talk to their family or friends. They choose to talk to me. Because of that, I am honored to lend a listening ear. That's all it takes. It can be a stranger at the gas station or at the grocery store. You never know when and where God is going to use you.

My pour comes from a strong place. That's one word that I would use to describe myself. I'm a team player. In this line of service, I have to keep a positive attitude. Even in the face of adversity, I have to maintain a professional posture. As strong and professional as I am, I had to learn how to take care of myself. I was helping people so much that I neglected myself. I'm talking about bad neglect. I ended up in the hospital with a blood pressure reading of 220/127. I was at high stroke-level potential. I'm teaching my clients about coping skills and self-care and I failed to take care of myself. I failed at practicing what I was preaching. Now, I practice self-care. I meditate. I listen to music, paint, and do things that I love to do. I love art work and I love poetry. I'm making sure to take care of myself with spa days and mental health days. One of the biggest personal helps comes through helping others. by helping others set short and long-term goals, I am able to heal more.

Here is a prime example of how I helped people in the middle of my storm. It was three days before Thanksgiving in 2021. I went to pay my rent but refused to put it into a night deposit box where overnight painters could see my money order fall to the floor. I didn't trust that so on that following Monday, I went to the office after taking off half of the day. They refused to take my money and decided to enforce the eviction law on me. I had too much to move in three days. So, I was calling people to come get new and slightly used stuff for their homes. I was being evicted, but still serving. That situation, along with more storms that I was dealing with, caused me to sink into a state of depression. All in all, it taught me to get prepared. Now, I'm preparing to purchase my home. That way, I won't have to deal with this anymore.

If I could leave anything with the readers of this chapter, it would be to remind you that "what's going on in the inside is more important than what's going on outside." What's happening on the inside of your (your health, your mind, and self-care) is more important. I want you to consider the process of healing and the process of self-care. What can you do to better yourself? It's an inside job. You have to pray. You have to meditate. You have to renew your thinking. Allow yourself to reflect and grow through tough seasons.

By pouring into others, teach them, encourage them and let them know that they are being heard.

Ashley S. Howell Pours

Email: ladya.s.h.91@gmail.com

My name is Ashley S. Howell, also known as Lady A. In my professional career, I have done a lot. I'm a manager at Circle K. I do sales for a wireless provider called Premium where we sell products and services for your major retailers. I previously did the same thing for Verizon. I also recruit for work-from-home jobs and my current position. I have participated in plus-size modeling, but due to some personal preferences, I've decided to do my own thing. In the plus-size modeling industry, I learned a lot. I'm not a confrontational person and I don't have to be in the spotlight. I prefer to be behind the scenes. I had a lot of friends in the modeling industry, but everything wasn't as it seemed. I'm confident in who I am, but I chose to step away from it to allow others to shine. Stepping away was a huge step for me. In my life, I've had to step away from companies, brands and names for personal reasons. In the end, I felt that if I could do this for them, I could do it for myself.

As a person, I like to be to myself. I'm very witty, and I love to laugh. One thing that many people don't know about me is that I have been homeless three times. Before I moved to Columbia, I was in between homes. I followed Brandy Henshaw, better known as Beasy Baybie, on social media. She always posts inspirational messages and a lot of times, she would share your posts. I reached out to her regarding my situation and she referred me to you and the Hannah House. By the time I heard about Hannah House, I made a friend and moved in with her. I stayed with her for about two years and then in 2020, I was able to stand on my own.

I left Columbia in March of 2022, but I was still driving back and forth from Louisiana every other weekend. That's like 12 hours. In life, when you have a desire to do something, you have to push through barriers to make it happen. I moved to Louisiana with only $12,000 and a new car. No family. No friends. I wanted to see what it would be like to do life on my own without the help of anyone. The decision to move wasn't all that easy. I was working at Kraft Heinz. Ironically, I was just offered two promotions. I turned one down and accepted the other because it offered more money and I had more leverage. I worked in that position for about two months and much like Casper, I was ghost. No one knew. My manager called and asked when I was coming back to work. I told them, "I'm not. I'm in another state." I rode with a co-worker to and from work. He was shocked to hear that I purchased and moved so fast. He thought I was dealing drugs. No sir. When I am determined to do something, I do it.

I love Louisiana, but I'm getting that urge to move again. I don't know where the next move will be. I don't think it will be to Columbia, but I am open to the upstate around Laurens and Greenville.

I'm a hustler at heart. I was raised by my grandmother. I was not raised by my biological parents. My mom's mother raised me because my mother and father were on drugs. And this was in their 30's. Being in my 30's, that makes me want to go harder. What kind of legacy do I want to carry on for my children? I taught my daughter at two years old how to wash dishes. Now, she's 14 and she know how to carry the house in my absence. My son is three and he knows how to clean the house. If you make a mess, he's going to get the vacuum and clean it up. At any given moment, something can happen. What are you able to do on your own before you ask for help?

I can remember as a child growing up that I saw my mother doing drugs one day. I cried so bad. She told me to walk away and I did. I never spoke about it because I lived with my grandmother. I never had a meaningful relationship with my mother until I was 14. Then, two months after my 15th birthday, she died in the hospital. That was hurtful to me because I was just getting to know her like I wanted to. My father and I still don't have a close relationship. So, it's just me, my kids, and my sister. I don't have the best relationship with her, and I am the baby sibling. I have 5 nieces and nephews and I definitely keep in contact with them. When they call, I come. When they call, I answer. When I come in town, it's all about the kids. I may not have much to talk about with the adults, but the kids are going to feel my love for them. I've created an extended family from previous co-workers and their families. Some have moved away, but we still keep in contact periodically.

Initially, I was hesitant about contributing to this project. All of the ladies have so many accolades and achievements that I don't have. However, I have worked for a long time to simply show up for myself. I'll be completing my degree in Psychology in a year. I'll be finishing my Medical Assistance in two months and then I will move on to Nursing. I've done all of this while holding down two jobs, being a mom and kickstarting my modeling career again. I had weight loss surgery last year followed by an issue with arthritis in my knees. Now, I'm about to get back into modeling. I want to show plus-size women that they can display beauty.

One of my biggest inspirations and a reason as to why I moved in 2022 is my dear Peggy Hemphill. She recently passed away. Many of the ladies on this project knew her very well. She was my spiritual sister. If I had something going on, I would call her. She told me that I was going to have a little chocolate boy. Mind you, I was still pregnant and I didn't even know what I was having. My son would always hide his face during ultrasounds. When my son was born, he was very light and red. Three days later, he was chocolate. I called her screaming, "You were spot on!" She pushed me to keep going. Everything she spoke into my life, I'm doing it now. She was my friend, but she was also like a second mom.

I've learned in life, that no matter what you have going on and even if you are late, keep showing up. I show up. For my kids. I show up. For this project. I show up. There have been times when I was overwhelmed about a situation and in my showing up, I found out that whatever was already fixed before I got there. I just showed up. That's what I've been doing and that's what I'm going to continue doing.

Valerie Yvette Simon Pours

Facebook: Valerie Yvette
Email: purposepusher@outlook.com
Instagram: @queenval66
Website: www.letstalkaboutitpublishing.net

My name is Valerie Yvette Simon. I am a victorious, young woman who has overcome many life adversities. I see myself as an encourager, an inspiration, and a woman of faith. Without my faith in God, I would not be here today. I am a purpose pusher. I even push the spectators that are haters. I noticed, that because of misplaced or misdirected admiration, individuals consider themselves in competition. They don't understand or overstand what I've gone through since overcoming a coma behind the scenes to even show up on a daily basis.

They see me smiling. They see me from any distance and they say, she's beautiful. I am a mother of four sons. If you total up the incarcerations of my sons, I've done almost 50 years in prison. They've done it physically, but I'm continuing to serve a sentence mentally and emotionally as a mother. I'm always pouring into others when I'm empty. No one seems to discern when I need some fuel. When I was approached about this project, I was very enthusiastic. I didn't know how I was going to get it done. I also sensed the end from the beginning. That means that I feel like there is going to be a great breakthrough through the release of this book for me. I'm a servant leader, but oftentimes I am misjudged and mishandled.

My faith in God keeps me standing. My life and faith are built on the word of God. It is the word of God that keeps me going. The word of God brought me from death to resurrection. I went from not being able to walk and talk to walking and talking again. There are days when I don't want to get up. There have been days when I regretted being resurrected from the coma. I have questioned as to why he brought me back. God has a purpose in me. Jeremiah 29:11 says, *"For I know the thoughts that I think toward you, saith the LORD, thoughts of peace, and not of evil, to give you an expected end."* That purpose allows me to rise up against the odds.

I found out a long time ago that life isn't easy. While parenting and being a mother, I made the struggle look easy to my children. I always had money, but I didn't have money like that. God has always been faithful to give me the provisions to make a way.

My pour is not a calling that I asked for. It's a choice. Yes, we have freewill. We can go out there and do whatever we want to do, but we have to choose the right path to take. We have to demonstrate spiritual discipline. As I get older and more mature, I understand that discipline is not a destination. It's a journey. Daily, I have to discipline myself. I have to discipline myself to pray. I have to discipline myself to worship. I have to discipline to maintain a heart posture of gratitude. If we aren't careful to discipline ourselves, we will sink into the very place that the people we serve are trying to get rescued from.

My pour is fueled through words of affirmation. There aren't any particular ones. I use whatever comes across in my daily journey. I work from home. Many times, I'm stuck in the office anywhere from 8-14 hours. During that time, I'm pouring and giving continuously. The bulk of my day is comprised of giving and serving. You can find me on the phone with a mother. You can find me encouraging a social worker. You can find me handling administrative duties or processing insurance. In all of my giving, I typically leave the office empty. My inspiration comes from watching a soap opera that I have been watching since I was a little girl with my grandmother. It's my way of escape. My happy place is the ocean. I love being near water. It allows me to see the waves and the immaculate power of God.

If I could offer encouragement to any woman who seeks community, a village, or a tribe of like-minded women, I would say, don't give up. Giving up is so easy. Your hardest test and trial comes with a lesson. It's almost like being in the wilderness. You can learn a lesson in the wilderness. Those spaces and places are opportunities to be prepared and for processes to be perfected. When you find yourself in a place of isolation, it's serving a purpose. You don't understand it. You can't define it, but it has a purpose. Isolation could be God's way of protecting you from something. Secondly, don't be afraid to celebrate yourself just because someone else doesn't celebrate you. Celebrate you. Treat yourself out and don't feel guilty for doing it. Lastly, don't allow anyone to minimize your victory. Don't allow anyone to minimize what you've had to overcome.

Celebrate your victory!

MICHELLE D. GARRETT POURS

Website: www.MichelleDGarrett.com

Instagram: Instagram.com/divamdgarrett

Facebook: Fb.com/michelledjohnsongarrett

My name is Michelle D. Garrett and I have power in my words. I'm going to just jump right in. I'm a blogger. When I first started blogging, I had no idea what a blog was. I had never read a blog. I didn't like being online. I was on social media and I was in a space where I had a story that needed to get out. I had a story that needed to be told. I knew that I wasn't alone in my feelings and thoughts. I knew that someone was sitting somewhere and feeling the same way and feeling like they were alone. I needed to get my words out there so I could connect with that audience. I figured that someone would stumble over my words one day and realize that they weren't crazy and someone shared their thoughts.

I can remember the exact timing of this writing. It was about 15 years ago because my child was a little over one. He was teething and running a fever. Finally, he fell asleep on the couch and I was wide awake. In that moment, I wrote my first blog for Divas With A Purpose. The name came out of nowhere. Everything I have done has been God-led. There was no other fashion or reason for it. All of the connections and all of the people that I have been privileged to work with over the years have been all because of God. Being able to tell my story has evolved into an entire business. It allows me the flexibility to be present for my family and when I need time for myself, I am able to do that too. My website is also up, providing income on a consistent basis. That's where making money in your sleep comes into play.

I have created a community for women in business who need support. I've encountered all types of women. I've been in their shoes too. I've been a single mother. There were times when my son had to come to work with me. If one of my employees called out, I had to step in. It's the weekend. Daycares are closed. My parents lived an hour away. I didn't have anyone that I really trusted in that area. After I did my own soul searching, the only resolve was to pack him up and take him to work with me. I dared my boss to say something. That was my mentality.

Sometimes, we are our biggest hindrances. I refuse to work with people that I want more for them than they want for themselves. Have you ever heard the question, "How bad do you want it?" I can't work with you if I want what you want more than you do. If you have made up in your mind that you can't do something, you're absolutely right. You're not going to be able to do it. I'm not going to fight with you. I'm not going to argue with you. I can't afford to spend unnecessary time and attention trying to do something that you have already made up your mind is going to be too difficult.

I've worked with a lot of people that have seen a lot of things not go right. In that, they are frustrated and hesitant to do new things. Oftentimes, I was the guinea pig for new technologies to see if they would work or not. You have to venture out to see where your people are. SnapChat was one for me. I couldn't stand SnapChat. It just wasn't for me, but there were some people who loved it and still love it. Then, there was ClubHouse. Some people do very well over there. For me, it was just a lot of excess chatter and noise. I gave ClubHouse an honest try. My mindset has always been in a mode to find a way for it to work. If it worked, it worked. If it didn't work, at least I had the experience.

My pour, my get up and go, and my show up gives me a sense of purpose. It makes me excited. When I come into my office, it's all mine. When I come into my office and close the door, I'm not a wife. I'm not a mother. I'm not a sister. I am Michelle. Many women are fighting to find their identity. I know that there is someone out there who needs to hear what I have to say. I am doing them a disservice by not sharing what has been placed on my heart. You never know. They may stumble across my blog. It may cause them to write that article. It may cause them to start that business. It may cause them to do something for themselves. It may bring joy to their heart. And when it does, that's my purpose fulfilled. That's the reason why I do what I do.

TIFFANY BELLAMY-LYLES POURS

Facebook: Tiffany Bellamy-Lyles

Email: tiffanyrbellamy84@gmail.com

My name is Tiffany Bellamy-Lyles. In times past, it was hard to define who I am. When someone asks the question who you are, most people respond with things that they do. God instructed me to respond in this manner. First and foremost, I am the daughter of a king. I am very God-fearing and I love the Lord. Everything that I am and everything that I do is centered around Christ. Like the song says, *"Jesus is at the center of it all"*. I like to tell people that I am a Jesus junkie. I am vivacious, full of life and I love every opportunity that God presents to me to be able to encourage and uplift others.

Growing up, I was considered part of the lower class. I mean the very low, lower class. I grew up in a two-parent household until I was about 6-years-old. I was exposed to domestic violence and an unstable household which caused us to move from place to place. I lived with my maternal and paternal grandparents. My paternal grandfather was a Reverend. He was a preacher. So I was introduced to all things church and God and he tried his best to embed that into my life. As a child, I didn't know anything about God and I didn't know anything about Jesus and I didn't really didn't want to know. I wanted to do things that I saw people in the world doing. What the people in the world were doing, looked more fun than going to church.

At the age of 15, reality hit like a ton of bricks when I became a mother. Life began to hit very fast. Then, at the age of 17, I became a mother again. Then, it happened at the ages of 18, 19, and 22. In the midst of all of that, I got married fresh out of high school. I was in a very toxic and abusive relationship. I ended up repeating a lot of the cycles that I saw in my family. There was no stability. I wanted stability and I vowed to myself that my children will never experience the things that I experienced. One bad thing about this vow was that it was not a Godly vow. That vow actually kept me in bondage in that marriage. My vow was for my children, but it didn't free me from that bad relationship.

When I was about 19-years-old, I was working at Wal-mart and this Pastor worked there too. He ministered to me about Jesus. This was completely different from the message, method and delivery that I was accustomed to from my grandfather. My grandfather talked about God in a way that made me scared of God. If I didn't do this, this was going to happen. If I didn't live like this, this was going to happen. This Pastor talked to me about the love of Jesus and what Jesus did for me. Every day was church at work. I would leave work and get into the Bible. The first book of the Bible that God led me to was the book of Job. The book of Job tells a story about a man who got knocked down over and over. God was trying to show me that this new journey will not always be easy. Everything isn't going to be peaches and cream. He took me to a book about trials and tribulations. In this story, God asked the enemy if he considered his faithful servant, Job. The enemy was reluctant to bother Job because God had placed a hedge of protection around Job. That encouraged me because if and when the enemy seeks to come my way, he has to get God's approval. God is all powerful and God is limitless. That's the type of God that I love and love to serve.

My marriage was filled with domestic violence. As a child, I grew up in the "keep your business at home" and "what happens at home, stays at home" era. From my mother, I learned, "I gotta make it work." In the process, I got pregnant with my daughter. I was still getting beat, and I was pregnant. There were no days off. There was no reprieve because I was pregnant. The abuse actually came up more. I'm working. I'm taking care of the bills. I'm getting promotions, and I was living in hell on earth. While pregnant, we had a house fire. My husband was at work. While asleep, I was awakened by a voice that said, "Tiffany! Get up!" and then there was a tug on my shoulder. I jumped up, looking around because it's just me and my kids in the house, but I smell smoke. What in the world?!?! My natural reaction caused me to run to the kitchen. No smoke. Then, I ran to my daughters' room. No smoke. Then, I came to my sons' room. I could feel the heat coming through the door. With one good tug of the door knob, it fell off. I found something to open the door. I had to get to my kids. When the door opened, the flames were at the door. My sons were talking towards me and they didn't have a burn anywhere on their body. That was the day that I realized that I was going to serve God for the rest of my life.

My decision to serve God didn't grant me clemency or immunity from the violence of my marriage. Remember? I was pregnant and I was still getting beaten. I went back to work three weeks after having my baby. One day, his mother came into the room and said that we need to hurry up and find somewhere else to live. Here comes the favor of God. Columbia Housing Authority called me and said that they had a house that was right around the corner from our last house. It was a three-bedroom home and it wasn't on Section 8. We moved the next week. The beating continued. It got so bad that my children started seeing it. During one argument, my daughter came in the room and gave him a hug. I believe that she did that to deter him from verbally abusing me. After that, he beat me again. I didn't have any clothes and I literally thought I was going to die. At a family gathering, he jacked me up so bad. My cousin saw it and told my brother. That caused a huge brawl. That wasn't to his advantage. Well, we all went home, and he gave me the same damage he received from my family.

Unless you are sick and tired of a situation, you'll never get out of that situation. I needed the help of God to help me. I asked God why He had me in that situation. I was expecting the "I won't put more on you than you can bare" message. God told me. I didn't put you in that. You put yourself in that. I asked God why he was letting me go through this. God replied, "You can't blame me for something that you didn't consult me about. You didn't consult me, but I will help you get out." And He did just what He said.

After all of that, God was still preparing me to pour. God took me through a new phase of healing. This healing came through telling my story. Through Fellowship Sisterhood at a church I was attending, I was afforded with an opportunity to share my story. Each week, there was another opportunity for me to share my story and tell about how God loved me in my mess. God kept me in my mess. Then, he turned my mess into a message that could minister to women who were going through what I had been through. Do you know how many times I heard, "I'm going through that" or "I needed to hear that" or "I know someone that is experiencing that". This is what got me to the point of being able to pour into women.

For those who are reading this glimpse and sample of my pour, I want to encourage you to trust God. If you don't know who God is, I want to encourage you to spend time with Him and seek a Bible-based church with sound doctrine that can teach you more about the gospel of Jesus Christ.

SHENEKA BOYLES POURS

Website: www.unapologeticallyno.com

Email: boylessheneka@gmail.com

My name is Sheneka Corbin Boyles. I am the CEo and Founder of Unapologetically No, LLC. I've dedicated my life to recovery, helping people set healthy boundaries for themselves. I am recovering from alcohol abuse. I have eight years of sobriety. I work at a well-known alcohol and substance abuse detox center here in Columbia, South Carolina. I've been in the dark for a long time, and I've come to the light. One of my goals is to help others who have experienced trauma issues. Those issues may have led them down the path of substance abuse or mental health issues. I want to encourage them and show them that they can recover. What we've been through doesn't define us.

My life issues started around the age of three. My parents divorced. My dad joined the military. My mom got remarried to my stepfather and he was molesting me. My parents had a very toxic relationship. It was a love-hate relationship. I had a lot going on in a short period of time. At the age of 14, I was pregnant with my first child. At the age of 16, I dropped out of high school. During that time, I was being physically and emotionally abused by my child's father. At the age of 19, I got married and then by the time I was 26, I was divorced with three children.

When I was married, I was considered uptight. My husband at the time would offer me drinks to calm me down or make me relax and loosen up. It started out as just fun. I always had a job and maintained a good job, but after work, I would have a drink here and there to wind down. After working 10-12 hours at work, I came to home to be a super mom and help with homework. In other words, I was a functioning alcoholic. Nobody knew it. I was still smiling and bubbly and I wore it all well until I had a car accident. It wasn't my car accident, but with this one I woke up in the hospital with a concussion. During that time, I decided to relocate to Virginia with my dad and my children. Out of embarrassment and shame, I checked myself into rehab at a facility in Florida. I left my kids with my father and stepmother. I was in rehab for 90 days before coming back to Columbia. I stayed in a transitional home for women for three months. I had to pick myself up by my bootstraps and do what I had to do to get myself back on track. Eight years later and I'm still standing. In the transitional home, they always encouraged us to not leave before the miracle happened and I didn't. I stayed right there. That concussion messed with me really badly. I didn't have to learn how to speak all over again. I did have to learn how to formulate my words. In my brain, my thoughts were mumbled and jumbled and it came out in my words.

Today, I am all about making me happy. I've always brought happiness and joy to people. I have come to the conclusion that if I am happy, I can do more for people. My happiness comes from a good place as opposed to smiling through pain. I don't have to drink to deal with my issues. I'm learning how to heal. I can take care of my mental health today. It's not the people like me that bother me. It's the people that are in denial about getting help that bother me. Those are the people that you should be concerned about. We have to eliminate the stigma that you are crazy if you go to the doctor and check on your mental health. I believe that you are crazy if you don't go to the doctor and check on your mental health. I actually take meds and that help me with anxiety and my moods. If you have to read, read. I you have to listen to music, listen to music. You have to go with what works.

I have learned to embrace and love myself. My pour involves teaching others to love themselves too. Find someone to talk to. That's free medicine. Find a safe place that you can trust. I am okay with being transparent. I'm not the first person to go to jail. I'm not the first person to get arrested or have a DUI. I'm not the first and definitely won't be the last to make a mistake. Your mind will have you thinking that you are the root cause of everything bad. Your mind will have you thinking that you are the target of billions of people in the world. That's not the case at all. The mind is a dangerous place to be by yourself. I tell people all of the time, it's okay to talk to someone. Talk about it. Talk about what's bothering you. If you can't find someone who you trust to talk about it, get a therapist. They make couches in all shapes, colors and sizes.

I really want to help young people and the next generation so they don't have to experience the bad side of life. In my line of work, I see young people are just trying. They are trying crack. They are trying molly's. I want to advocate for young people so they don't have to go that route. Young people today resort to drugs and alcohol and once they start, it's hard to stop. One of the biggest misconceptions about hangovers is that you need another drink to get over it. Alcohol is liquid dope. Your body is trying to get right because it has become dependent on the alcohol. Then, the worst thing to do is to go cold turkey. That can turn your body against itself and you can have a seizure or die from it. A lot of people don't understand that. I believe that alcohol should have a warning on commercials just like cigarettes.

I want my life to be a life of service. When I got to Virginia, I started at American Red Cross. I feel like it is my duty to demonstrate and show people what recovery looks like. Without God's grace and mercy, I would be nothing. Even worse, I would have been dead. I couldn't have done it without God and the people that were there for me. Because of that, I need to be there for people. It's all about reaching back and helping somebody else. If I talk to 100 people and one person changes their life, my job is done. Then, the cycle continues. All it takes is one. After that one impacts another, we end up changing the world.....one person at a time. I love the life that I am living today. I love myself today. I love the people that I encounter on a daily basis. I am so spiritually in tune with the universe. People are attracted to my light whether I find them or they find me. Life is about being happy and making people happy.

My life's mission is to continue doing what I am doing. I ask God for guidance everyday. He places me where He wants me. I don't move without his instruction and direction. I'm working on my business. I'm working on elevating myself by gaining more knowledge. As I grow, I am able to pour into more and women. We are in a great season in our lives. There are some great opportunities out there to network and engage with other people. We come in different shapes, colors and sizes, but we are more alike than we are different. I love seeing women, and more specifically, black women show up for themselves. We have our own authentic and genuine stories. We're handling business. We're standing on business and I love to see it.

Kathy H. English Pours

Facebook: Kathy Holloway-English

Email: kathyvernell61@aol.com

My name is Kathy H English. I was born and raised in Washington, DC. I am the baby of the family. I'm the baby on my dad's side and the only child on my mom's side. I moved to South Carolina in 1991 with my first husband. When he passed away, it was me and my daughter until I got married again, which I shouldn't have done. That's another story for another day, month or year. Pick one! We've been separated since 2016. So, now I live with my daughter. I have three kids, two bonus children and four grandchildren. I decided to go back to school in 2020. I received my Bachelor's Degree in Legal Studies. I received my Master's degree in Healthcare Administration and I am currently working on my doctoral degree in Healthcare Administration with an emphasis on disparities in African American communities. When my husband and I separated, I wanted to do something different. When your marriage comes to an end, part of you wants to end too, but I couldn't do it. I looked at my grandson. He has successfully been through eight ear surgeries. If he can go through that, I can go through my situation. I want to teach my grandchildren that they can do anything and nothing is impossible. I want to turn all of this education into a career opportunity that is either a director or administrator for a nursing home or a long care facility. It is imperative to know your benefits and the benefits and coverage for your elderly family members. If you don't, things can go haywire.

Growing up started with both of my parents. Then, they separated when I was about seven. I lived with my dad after that. My mom says that I was brainwashed into staying with him. I don't remember. I do remember being with her almost every weekend. I was over her house just as much as I was with my dad. I was born with spina bifida. In the 60's there was no cure for it. I didn't learn to walk until I was four years old. I think that is where I got my compassionate side from – the struggle. I know what it is to struggle to do the simplest things like walk and run. I know what it is to be laughed at and picked on. My dad used to tell me that I was too soft-hearted. That's just who I am. That really came into play with my step-daughter. I have raised her since she was three years old. When my husband and I separated, he didn't want to take her with him and I refused to let her go into the foster care system. I have raised her as if she was my own child.

Have you looked at an obituary or funeral program? There is always a birth date and a death date. You don't have a choice in your birth date. Only a few have a choice in their death date. But that dash? You have a lot of control over what happens during that dash. I want to be a part of something where I can learn and be mentored. I want something to be said about my dash. I want to pass something on to the next generation. My main goal is to show women my age that it is never too late to start over. Things may have fallen apart at the beginning or along the way, but you can pick yourself up. Your story is not necessarily just for you. It could be for the person that you pass in the grocery store. They may be going through what you have already gone through. I just want to give back because so much has already been given to me.

If you are reading this chapter, I want you to know that I have overcome some big challenges in my life. I've been knocked down, but I got back up. I was torn apart, but God put me back together again. Let me be more specific. In both of my marriages, I experienced domestic violence. The second marriage was worse than the first. I wanted to get out. I told God that I didn't have the strength or will to get out of the relationship. I told God that if He wanted me out of the relationship that He was going to have to take me out of it. Three months later, we lost our home. I've had health challenges. I was walking around with blood sugar levels of 500 and 600 for over five years. I've had three stints placed in my heart in three years. I've been in seven car accidents in 10 years, and none of them were my fault. After all that and all that I've been through, I'm still here. According to Philippians 4:13, "I can do all things through Christ which strengtheneth me." If I could do it at my age, you can do it too.

Dr. Ronda Stinson Boyd Pours

Email: flowwithronda@gmail.com

I am Dr. Rhonda Stinson Boyd. I am a mother, a grandmother, a wife, and much like many of the women you have read about in this book, I wear many hats. As a nonprofit owner, I am a philanthropist. I've worked in the court system and in corporate America. Seven years ago, I was able to leave corporate America. When that job came to an end, my husband encouraged me to figure out my next move because I wasn't going to be driving up and down the road.

Everything that I do is centered around generational wealth. From my nonprofit organization to banking and insurance, I seek to help women create, keep and pass generational wealth. Along with teaching about generational wealth, I invest and teach people how to get passive income in different areas of life. I am the President for the Columbia, South Carolina Black Women Invest. This is a new chapter that brings black women together to learn, share and experience the plethora of open doors for black women to be able to invest. We have chapters all over the country.

My inspiration comes from the work of my nonprofit. My organization teaches kids how to be entrepreneurs and how to manage money. We have a project called Passion 2 Pay, where we teach kids about how the things they love to do can actually pay them. There is a mantra that says, "if you love what you do, you'll never work a day in your life." I believe that your hobbies and pastimes can pay you.

This next opinion may get me in trouble. Here we go. I don't believe every child is meant to go to college. In some cases, school may be required such as in careers for the medical or law field. However, I don't think it is logical to go to school for years and to come out with loads of debt. If we didn't have so much debt, we would have more wealth to invest. I'm not talking against school or education, but without a plan to pay the loans back or if the kid doesn't have an end game after college, we are setting up the next generation to fight an uphill debt battle. That's not fair.

I try my best to help people with additional career opportunities in real estate and real estate investing. Even through insurance policies, you can have another avenue of passive income with interest that is compounded. The Bible teaches about leaving an inheritance for your children's children. It's a proven fact that wealth is lost within four generations. You can have a million dollars, but in four generations all of that money can be gone.

My pour thrived in one of the most challenging seasons in the history of the word: Covid. Everyone one was home. I found this book called "What Do Billionaires Do?" by Garrett Gunderson. This completely changed the trajectory of my thought process. When you think about generational wealth, that has been going on for hundreds of years. Building community has been going for so many years. It's not new to many but it was new to our community. Most think that final expense policies are the saving grace. That policy leaves nothing for the next generation. Most people have the warped mentality that "if I had to work for it, my children are going to have to work for it too." Do you know that I reached out to Garrett Gunderson? I never heard back from him, but I believe in making connections and building business relationships. I wanted to know how he was doing what he does. I was looking for a company that was doing what I do. While in Texas, I was walking to the store daily for exercise. One day, while walking, I received a phone call from a stranger that sought to connect with me. When you are sincerely seeking greatness and success in a given area, God will send the people and the resources to you.

Through my philanthropic and community efforts, I want to help facilitate conversations about one of the most shameful and prideful topics. This four-letter word is synonymous with a curse word. That word is debt. All of us have it. Many of us are concerned about it, but none of us are talking about it. We go on vacations with our families and friends. We go to dinner. We host family functions and we don't have the conversation that can change the lives of so many people. When the bills come in, we put them on the shelf and let them collect dust. We don't like talking about money.

My kids, my grandkids, and the kids in the center inspire me to want to do more. We, as adults, must do our part to educate the next generation. It starts with communication. The last book that I wrote was called "Investing Made Easy". This book was initially for adults, but two chapters in, I noticed that I was more concerned with the children. I have a workbook in the middle of the book. I tried to re-direct the subject matter for the book back to the adults, but the assignment to educate the next generation just made more sense to me. We have to talk to our kids about what's going on in the world. My kids are like this light that gives me the energy to do what I do and to continue the work.

Pouring has been hard for me. I had to find my voice in this. I was out there talking about Infinite Bank and Family Bank. These things have been out there forever, but our community was not talking about it. I had to remind myself that people didn't know about this. When people don't know about something, they reject it. I couldn't stop talking about it because if I did, they still wouldn't know about it. We should be the ones that hold the wealth. We should be the lenders and not the borrowers. Being wealthy and being rich look different for different people. Some people want to be able to get up and go and do what they want to do, but they don't have a lot of money to do that. I am called to get a message to the generation that is behind us. That generation will need options and a leg up to do what they are called to do. I believe that all of our callings are intertwined. If I decide to stop because someone tells me no, I will hold up someone else. If I stop because I don't see the movement, I will hinder someone else's progress. That's why I pour. I understand my role. I pour in the face of adversity. I pour with the hope that people will explore additional avenues for creating wealth. People will talk about what should be done all day long, but they are reluctant to share how to get it done. I want to share that lesson. I want to help people learn how to do it and how to understand what they are doing.

My method is not a get-quick scheme. This new culture wants the microwave life. They want things quick. This is a night an overnight success story. You have to put in the work, and you have to be patient through the process. One of the first questions that I asked when I sit down with people is, "what are your goals?" Then, I ask, "when can you start?" The hardest step in making progress in anything is to start. If you don't start or if you don't know where you are going, you'll never make any progress.

I have an acronym that I use in my teachings and it's called M.O.V.E. **M** is for **M**ake a decision. You have to make a decision in knowing where you want to go. Making a decision changes your direction. When you make the right decision, doors will begin to open. The **O** is for **O**wn your results or **O**wn your truth. You have to own where you're at right now. Your previous decisions and actions have determined where you're at right now. That doesn't mean you have to stay there, but you do have to recognize where you're at. If you're in debt, you have to do something about it. The **V** is **V**isualization. You have to visualize where you want to go. Oftentimes, people can't see past tomorrow for the next hour. When you visualize, it gives you hope. It gives you hope for a bigger future. Where do you want to be five years from now? What would you love your life to be like three years from now? Visualize every day. The **E** is for **E**xpectation. People pray all the time. They pray for this and they pray for that, but they lack an expectation that it can happen. You have to decree and declare: this will happen for me. I expect to be here in three years. I expect my life to be completely different. When you focus on those things and understand and you have that picture of hope in your mind, you'll create an environment of expectation. You wake up differently. You show up differently. You face obstacles differently. Ultimately, you'll be able to pour differently.

ABOUT THE VISIONARY

KIWAN N. FITCH

Kiwan N. Fitch - Entrepreneur, Published Author/CoAuthor of 10 books, Speaker, Film Producer, Playwright, Professional Development Coach, and so much more. Kiwan owns multiple businesses. She is a gifted and highly skilled Visionary with over twenty years of experience in Non-Profits Organizations, Leadership, Business, and Entrepreneurship.

She is the CEO of EmPOWERment Corp., LLC. a company she created to expand her work with women and families in transition. To date, the EmPOWERment Corp LLC has produced 10 books, 6 live stage productions in South Carolina, 2 live productions in New Jersey, Co-produced 2 live productions in Louisiana, and has performed at several local events including the IMARA Woman Magazine Health

Tour (2015, 2016, and 2017), The Ms. Born Natural Pageant (2016) and the Big DM's 2015 and 2016 Women's EmPOWERment event at the Convention Center.

In 2018 Ms. Fitch launched the Journey Towards Purpose Program as a part of the J2P Global Institute LLC. With this platform she offers personal development courses in a live and online format. J2PGI also offers individual and group coaching in the area of Business, Nonprofit organizational leadership, and Business Incorporation. The institute is a curriculum-based program that Certifies Purpose Coaches. To date, Kiwan has certified over 50 Purpose Coaches in North and South Carolina, Pennsylvania, New Jersey, Florida, Georgia, Illinois, Alabama, Tennessee, Texas, and London England.

To date, J2P Global Institute LLC has become a premier company that primarily focuses on assisting individuals with skills, resources, and development needed to achieve their business and personal goals. Ms. Fitch and her team offer brand development, courses, conferences, and one on one coaching sessions. J2P is the "Go To" for Nonprofit Leadership specifically birthing new nonprofit organizations from concept to 501c3.

As purpose would have it; in 2018 Kiwan joined the management team at Hannah House, a transitional housing facility for women and children, which is a part of Christ Central Ministries. She served as the Director of the Transitional Housing Program until August 2023.

Embracing her new MBA credentials, Kiwan took her management skills to Senior Living Apartments. There she served as the licensed property manager for 2 apartment communities that serve nearly 100 senior citizens.

She also sits on the board of directors of nonprofit organizations that serve women and families.

Kiwan is the mother of 3 sons, 2 daughter in loves, 3 grandsons, and 2 granddaughters. Hailing from Jersey City, NJ Kiwan made Columbia,

South Carolina their home in 2010. Kiwan is a South Carolina Notary. She has a Bachelor of Arts degree in Sociology from New Jersey City University. She has a Master's degree in Business Administration from Walden University. She is also pursuing a Community Chaplaincy Certification from Christ Central Ministries Institute.

Kiwan N. Fitch, MBA

Journey Towards Purpose Global Institute, LLC

CoachK@J2PGlobalInstitute.com

www.SheisCoachK.com